A BREATH OF FRESH PRAYER

A Breath of Fresh Prayer

SUE BARNETT

KINGSWAY PUBLICATIONS

EASTBOURNE

Front cover photo: The Image Bank

British Library Cataloguing in Publication Data

Barnett, Sue
A breath of fresh prayer.
1. Prayer
I. Title
248.32

ISBN 0–86065–904–6

Printed in Great Britain for
KINGSWAY PUBLICATIONS LTD
1 St Anne's Road, Eastbourne, E Sussex BN21 3UN by
Richard Clay Ltd, Bungay, Suffolk.
Typeset by J&L Composition Ltd, Filey, North Yorkshire

Contents

Acknowledgements

This book was written in the twenty-fifth year of our marriage. It is dedicated to the people who mean the most to me: Doug, Stephen and Duncan, and our parents, Ralph and Edith Raymond and Doug and Min Barnett.

Thank you to Belinda Hill for her work on the manuscript, and to Sally Beale for her illustrations.

1

Help!

My introduction to the breathtaking world of skiing catapulted me back into the precarious days of childhood. My moods fluctuated from intoxicated excitement to indescribable exhaustion. The daring streak in my nature resurfaced, only to be plunged headlong into embarrassment and raw insecurity. My ego wasn't the only area bruised!

The Christian life can be equally exhilarating and bewildering if we don't grasp that it is a demanding partnership we embark on with God himself. No longer a distant deity, we enter a life-changing relationship with the person who knows and loves us most. The hand that carved creation shaped us in our mother's womb, and through this developing relationship we can face everything that life offers. From failure to success, anticipation to disappointment, peace and pain, tragedy and triumph. All the inevitable contrasts of human experience are confronted and channelled with life's divine managing director. Relationship with God is crucial and of vital importance to life and its daily outworking.

Prayer is not a reluctant routine or a rigid rule, but a voyage of discovery into a world of close communication with our Creator.

Back to the nursery slopes! As I burst forth onto the snowy scene, heavy with boots, skis and apprehension, my ears were ringing with kindly advice. One pearl of wisdom stayed with me as I tumbled and gasped my way up and down the mountains: 'Stick close to your guide and instructor!' Our instructor proved to be Raymond, a tanned French ski expert who knew the mountains inside out and had been skiing as long as he had been walking. In the two days that followed, I clung tenaciously to that advice. Hanging on to his every word, my skis literally followed the imprint of his tracks. Each warning, change of direction, and instruction was picked up immediately and acted upon. Copying his every twist and turn, my confidence was growing again—literally by leaps and bounds! Gazing at the beauty of the surroundings, my skis wandered onto fresh snow, unmarked and crisp. Others took my place behind Raymond and I thrilled to my new-found skill and independence. Weaving between trees and other skiers, I gathered speed, the wind ringing in my ears. Suddenly the sky and snow were somersaulting around me, and I landed in a crumpled heap with my skis at painful angles!

Experts swished past me, oblivious of my dilemma. The slopes were crawling with fallen beginners, and I was no exception. All alone, and very damp, I longed for the security of those ski tracks right behind Raymond. His words of encouragement and guidance were silent. I had abandoned my close contact with the expert, and as a result was grovelling in the depths of icy slush instead of skimming the heights with the others. Weariness swept over me and I determined to give up the whole idea and experience of skiing. I was sinking further into my damp depression when, with a magnificent spray of snow, Raymond came to a halt beside me. Without a word he hauled me to my feet, and taking my hand firmly in his, guided me expertly down the mountain.

A life of prayer is so similar to that mountain slope. The many who are experiencing and enjoying God's unique gift of a close relationship with him seem few in comparison with those fallen beginners who litter the paths, or those who remain at the foot of the mountain, observing all the activity, but never committing themselves to getting involved. Life is no optional pastime. Knowing God personally and communicating with him is as essential to life itself as air is to breathing and snow is to skiing.

'He who has the Son has life. He who does not have the Son of God does not have life' (1 Jn 5:12). That is a sweeping statement! If what the Bible says is true, then this verse means Jesus, the Son of God, is a person to be checked out and that our relationship with him is a priority.

It was the word 'Jesus' which first captured my attention as a toddler. The discovery that the last three letters of this name were the first three letters of my name did not seem to impress my Sunday school teacher! She thought my frantically waving hand meant that I was going to produce some spiritual gem that would help her with her unimaginative story telling, and my discovery was discarded with impatience. The word cropped up continually throughout my childhood. Just a name, something I sung about, prayed about in church, and saw in picture books. It seemed a great excuse for Easter eggs at Easter and for presents at Christmas time.

Standing proudly as a red-kilted archangel Gabriel, I had recited the following words one Christmas without making any world-shattering discovery about life: 'Unto you is born this day in the City of David, a Saviour which is Christ the Lord' (Lk 2:11).

However it was this name, part of my home and security as I grew up, which caused a major disturbance to my life in the important teen years. Doubt, fear and concern swept through me every time it was mentioned. My avoiding tactics became imaginative and frequent as I desperately, but unsuccessfully, tried to blot out any possibility of confronting that name. It was a bewildering battle, fought within, with no one aware of my struggle. I hated the name of Jesus because of the inexplicable disruption it had brought to my otherwise happy life.

A very similar upset resulted from the Second World War. Born into a London family, my father had been posted to Egypt shortly after my birth. Daddy was just a name and a black-and-white photo on the piano, and for three glorious years I was the centre of my mother's attention. My two sisters and a neighbourhood full of women were at my beck and call; I had no experience of men in my contented little world. (We did have a milkman. However, he called at four in the morning and I couldn't build much of a relationship at that time!)

The disruption came in January 1946 when Mum announced, 'We are going to meet Daddy!' The photo on the piano wasn't sufficient for my mother this time, and my confusion mounted as I was decked out in a dress instead of dungarees! It was evident that my usually mature and attentive mum was preoccupied and her excitement bewildered me as we piled into a London taxi. Waterloo Station, at the best of times, is not a peaceful haven. This was 1946, the age of the steam engine, and troops were returning triumphantly to thousands of waiting families. The explosion of steam and clatter of engines were all drowned out by the high-pitched excitement of hundreds of women. I clung to my mum's hand, knee high to them all. As a trained nurse and sister, my mother never ran. Imagine the panic in my little heart when I was left rooted to my knee-crowded spot, watching the back view of my mum running away from me and flinging herself into the arms of a man! I wasn't used to men, and certainly not strapping six-footers who bore down upon me. Two gigantic arms reached out towards me and hands, more like bunches of bananas, wrapped around me. The deepest voice I had ever heard boomed into my ear, 'You must be Sue. I'm Daddy. I've loved and missed you so much and I am coming to live in your house. Isn't that lovely?'

My mother had tried desperately to prepare me for this moment. But how do you explain to an active toddler, who rarely stayed still for five seconds, that the reason for her secure and happy home was because of a strange man in a foreign country who loved and cared for her? How do you tell her that the roof over her head is because he sent home every penny of his army pay for her comfort? And then, I ask you, how do you present her with the precious facts of life that her very existence is because of him? As far as I was concerned he was an intruder, and my little life had turned upside down!

It has taken a lifetime to reach an adult relationship with my father, who is now an active eighty-year-old. Because of his patient love and understanding, years of stilted communication and long periods of uncomfortable silence have been transformed into a relationship that has affected my approach to life and all other relationships.

So what is this disturbing similarity between the name of Daddy and the name of Jesus? It was clearly no problem for a toddler when Daddy was just a name and a lifeless photograph. I enjoyed all the benefits of this distant, impersonal relationship without lifting a finger. All the hassles commenced when I discovered Daddy was a real, live person with emotions and desires. He wanted to talk to me and hear my voice in conversation, however childish, and this turn of events had a lasting impression on me. I was thrown headlong into the mysteries of a father–daughter relationship, without any warning or preparation.

Ideal parent–child relationships evolve over years of close proximity and tangible love and understanding. The World Wars brought separation, families were torn apart and many relationships, unlike mine, were never healed. The invasion of sin into our world has had more far-reaching effects than all the wars put together. The most important relationship of all time was blown apart—that between men and women and their Creator.

As the twentieth century accelerates towards its close in what seems an avalanche of violence and fear, what hope is there as we approach the twenty-first century? There is no hope without God. When God, clothed as his Son Jesus, allowed himself to be brutally nailed to a rough tree, he voluntarily entered the ultimate result of sin—death. He who was sinless did not have to choose that route, but in order to smash once and for all the power of sin in our lives, he absorbed the whole horrific catalogue of sinful actions and attitudes into his body, a mental and spiritual agony that far outweighed the physical pain. As he passed through death itself with this horrendous load, he smashed its painful hold on the world and opened up a way for escape through his resurrection power over sin and death.

Without this relationship with God, we are deprived of spiritual life. We have all the human skills of discovery, invention and achievement, but no divine director to channel that unleashed power. We build houses, but fail to build homes; we master the art of refrigeration, but can't cool tempers. We purify water and air, but can't purify our minds. Power and electricity are generated, but not love and understanding. We achieve the test tube babies, while the figure for child abuse rises alarmingly. Our rocket ships are discovering the secrets of the universe, but have completely missed the source. The discovery I made in my teens was that the source of all life is a person who can be known, the Lord Jesus Christ. He isn't just a name, a convenient idea for festivities, or a secure place to go on Sundays. There is literally more to the word 'Jesus' than meets the eye! As with my father, I had been enjoying the gifts of a distant, impersonal relationship which supplied me with physical life and growth, without enjoying the full potential of all these areas through a committed, close relationship with a real, live person.

'How sweet the name of Jesus sounds' are the stirring words of an old and loved hymn written by John Newton. That name certainly held no sweetness for me as I fought and struggled against it for two long years. The mysterious battle came to an end one day in the 1950s. These were the days of so-called freedom of expression, love and morality. Right in the middle of them I found the true freedom that only Jesus can bring when he breaks into the circle of sin and death with all its accompanying sadness. Instead of hearing that now dreaded name, I came face to face with a living God, made understandable and visible in the life of an ordinary young woman. Through her he spoke the words found in Revelation 3:20—'Here I am! I stand at the door and knock. If anyone hears my voice and opens the door, I will come in and eat with him and he with me.' The two years of fighting this unknown voice, and hearing the incessant knocking which drew my attention back to a person, not a name, suddenly made sense. Without realising it, the adventure of a lifetime had only just begun. With struggling hesitancy I muttered in my mind, 'Is this really you, Jesus? Are you actually speaking to me? Is everything in the Bible about you true? Are you alive and able to enter my day-to-day experience?' With this growing realisation the fighting began to recede, and without fully understanding what I was doing, I simply asked God to enter my life and show me what it was all about. In that moment I prayed for the very first time. Before I had known about God, I had prayed and sung about him, I had listened to stories about him. In those few seconds I actually spoke to him. I stepped out in a moment of bewildered searching, and in a blind request of faith I discovered the life-giving, life-changing power of prayer.

Workout session

(1) Write down the miracle of how you first entered into a relationship with Jesus. Yes—go on, have a go! Even if you have known him for some time or for just a few days, capturing it on paper can clarify and confirm what God has done. It can also show us more about ourselves and God. Until I wrote down my teenage meeting with God thirty years after it happened, God did not show me the parallel between my experience with the name 'Daddy' and the name of Jesus.

(2) Memorise the last part of John 10:10 'I have come that they may have life and have it to the full.' Practise applying this verse to all situations of life.

(3) List the areas in your life that could do with fresh enthusiasm. Eg, my marriage, my job, the essay due in tomorrow, my children, exams, responsibilities in church and community.

(4) Ask God for that freshness and fullness of life that can help you face something specific today or this week.

(5) If you are just exploring the facts about Jesus or have already entered a relationship with him, read Luke chapter 9 and Luke 10:25–41, finishing with chapter 11 verse 1 in preparation for the next chapter.

Group activity

(1) 'Anyone who wants to follow me must . . . keep close to me' (Lk 9:23, TLB). Share with each other practical ways in which you can keep close to someone you can't see physically, ie, be in a position to *hear* him or her. Read the Bible.

(2) In pairs. Without using their name, describe a well-known figure in politics, sports or your locality, and ask your partner to identify that person.

(3) Describe what God means to you. This may involve reading your testimony or, if you find it easier to talk than to write, share either the first time you met Jesus or a recent experience of his love and care. If you are just exploring the facts, explain why and how your exploration is going.

(4) In your pairs, God has heard your conversation and thoughts. Welcome him into your group and pray for each other, and for your relations with him and each other. Just be yourselves and keep your prayers short.

A prayer of commitment is at the back of the book for those who want to start the journey of a lifetime.

Recommended reading

Ian Coffey, *You Can Know God* (SU/Saltmine Publication)

Doug Barnett, *You Can Be Sure You Are a Christian* (SU/Saltmine Publication)

James I Packer, *Knowing God* (Hodder and Stoughton)

2

Love at First Sight

Following my painful gymnastics on the ski-slopes, I never let Raymond, our ski-instructor, out of my sight. Affectionately known as the 'red blob', we scoured the dazzling snow scene for his bright red ski-suit throughout our lessons. After six exhilarating days we were very sad to say goodbye to our French friend on whom we had become so dependent. From sport to science, politics or prose, accounting or agriculture, cooking or communicating, our process of learning all these skills is helped or hindered by those who teach us. Whether parent, teacher, friend or personal instructor, our success or failure in all the lessons of life depends on the quality of our training and our ability to learn.

Take history, a subject I dreaded at school. The lessons held no life, and the boring dates and monotonous catalogue of events from the past matched the tedious teacher who delivered them. I emerged from every frustrating forty minutes, and eventually into adult life, with a total lack of interest in the past and no knowledge of its significance for the present and future. Gratefully discarding all thoughts of dates and dusty exercise books, along with school and homework, it was a few years later that I walked the streets of London revelling in its history. Why the transformation? It was so simple! Holding my hand and enjoying my company, was a young man who was later to become my husband. As we tramped the otherwise grey pavements, he brought to life the drab figures and events of the past in a way that captured my imagination.

Take the Monument. The boring grey stone became alive with memories of the horrific Great Fire of London in 1666 which it commemorates. Doug's graphic descriptions reflected his love of history and breathed life into the dry facts I had reluctantly 'picked at' with my teacher. The Tower of London throbbed with past and present life, the White Tower's silent walls hiding the secrets of the death of two young princes and many prisoners of the past. All this and so much more intrigued me as history leapt into life and changed my whole view of the City of London.

For many years after my introduction to Jesus as a real live person, prayer was an optional extra, an activity you did as a Christian, like reading your Bible and going to church. In times of trouble I was more aware of my need to call upon outside help, but prayer was a routine that if not forgotten, was boring and tedious. It was associated with people standing, sitting or kneeling, shut in on themselves with eyes closed, hands clenched and a bowed, depressed posture. It seemed to have little relationship with the communication of lively people, eyes locked in concentration, giving the whole of their

personality and attention to one another. A deep dissatisfaction set in as I sought to live this Christian life
that some said was so exciting. I longed for Jesus to take
my hand along the path of life and show me the secrets of
communication with him. In my search, I started to read
the first four books of the New Testament, where we see
Jesus walking this earth.

I started in Luke's Gospel, making my way rapidly
through the familiar nativity story to watch with fascination Jesus as a twelve-year-old boy, sitting with rapt
attention as he listened and asked questions of the
teachers of the temple court. His hunger for knowledge
and communication was contagious. I read on, eager to
watch Jesus in every situation, as he walked and talked
with people. The excitement mounted as John the Baptist
tells of the Messiah who is to come. Along with the
crowds gathered in the wilderness, I could well imagine a
grand, distant figure to be worshipped from afar rather
than entering into intimate conversation with. 'John
answered them—but one more powerful than I will
come, the thongs of whose sandals I am not worthy to
untie' (Lk 3:16).

The crowds would have been familiar with the image
of a terrifying God as depicted in Exodus 19:20—'And
the Lord said to Moses, "Go down and warn the people
so they do not force their way through to see the Lord
and many of them perish".' John's words would only
emphasise a God who was unapproachable.

As, in my imagination, I stood in the crowd on the
banks of the Jordan listening to John the Baptist, I
noticed an ordinary man step into the water like many
others before him. He waded his way down to John the
Baptist to be baptised. This is no terrifying, unapproachable deity. This is no boring figure from history. This is
Jesus Christ! Right at the commencement of his ministry
he is praying. It is while he is talking to his Father that

we see a white dove fly down and rest on him. At this moment, John's face is a picture. In John's Gospel we read a parallel story of this same event. There John the Baptist says, 'I would not have known him, except the One who sent me to baptise with water told me, the man on whom you see the Spirit come down and remain is he who will baptise with the Holy Spirit. I have seen and I testify that this is the Son of God!' (Jn 1:33–34). Remembering the powerful impact of 1 John 5:12—'He who has the Son has life; he who does not have the Son of God does not have life—I realised how much I had underestimated this powerful life.

I closely followed every word, move and turn of Jesus as I devoured Luke's Gospel. With a need more powerful than that on the ski slopes when I searched for our instructor, I scoured the Scriptures for a sight of Jesus. I hung on to his every word and studied his every reaction. With the imagination and senses that God had given me, I visualised the scenes, smelt the sea, and heard the crowds' commotion. I walked with him on his journeys between towns. I withdrew with him and the disciples after days of hard work and nights without sleep to see with mounting exasperation, the approaching crowd seeking out our hiding place. I watched with amazement the unreserved welcome Jesus gave them and the untiring way he helped and healed them. I entered into the debate with him when he posed the question to his disciples: 'Who do the crowds say I am?' (Lk 9:18).

Wending my way through Scripture, verses leapt into life as communication with Jesus was so direct and real. Whether relaxing over meals, walking through cornfields, or sailing in fishing boats, communication with the Son of God was close, clear and full of variation. It brought a depth of relationship that continually kept me seeking for his company, inspiration and reassurance.

Take Peter, for example—a rough, rugged fisherman;

a man of action and constant motion. Jesus so captivated him that he dropped everything to accompany and support him in his world-changing mission. A leader of tough men, he followed Jesus without question. Full of forthright demands and flashes of inspiration, it was he who delivered the power-packed revelation, 'You are the Christ of God!' (Lk 9:20).

Both Martha, a busy hostess, and Mary, her quiet listening sister, were hungry for Jesus' company and words of wisdom. Wild extroverts, reserved introverts, studious doctors and scheming tax collectors were just a few of the people who were irresistibly drawn to the quiet authority of this man Jesus. What was the secret behind this powerful, unique life? Those closest to Jesus readily followed his practical advice as they set out on preaching missions or controlled the masses for an open-air meal. They watched in wonder as he quietly but authoritatively healed the sick and taught with such clarity and vivid illustration. They admired his stamina and lively concentration throughout his long, action-packed days and nights.

As they shared and studied Jesus' life, they could have asked for seminars in storm control on Galilee or training in crowd control at picnics. Healing, time management, story-telling and parable performance could have well been on their agenda for further instruction. Surprisingly, not one of these subjects was asked for. Instead those who were in touch with the visible, physical Jesus, touched on what was at the heart of that incredible life with their direct request, 'Lord, teach us to pray!' They observed that everything about this powerful life hinged on his relationship with his Father. From his baptism, Jesus prayed his way through forty days and nights of fasting and temptation. Whether in solitary places or in crowds, in private homes or public synagogues, in company or alone, along roadways or through the countryside, Jesus was in constant contact with God his Father. The effect was dynamite, and the disciples were hungry for the secret. Prayer, as seen in Jesus, was a dynamic way of life. Dynamic life is a way of prayer!

Still reading Luke, I couldn't get further than verse one of chapter 11. If the disciples, who spent more time with Jesus than anyone, had to ask him to teach them how to pray, surely this should be a simple, ongoing request of mine—'Lord, teach *me* to pray!' I had never thought to ask Jesus personally. I assumed that as a Christian you prayed, read your Bible and went to church. It seemed like asking for the obvious, but the simple request stopped me in my tracks, and I had no desire to read further.

'Lord, teach me to pray!' These words dogged my footsteps, but were not uttered from my heart. My prayer requests continued in habitual style, rounded off automatically with the words, 'If it be your will.' But surely here was a simple, direct prayer that needed no such closing phrase? It was an obvious burning desire of a God who created relationship to teach me to understand and communicate with him. Why had I taken him and my relationship with him for granted for so long? Was this the reason for my dry dissatisfaction? God didn't just want to teach me the mechanics of prayerful repetition, but the miracle of a personal relationship. The simple difference between formal conversation and falling in love! A relationship that revolutionises and reshapes the whole of life.

As breath and breathing are vital to physical life and fitness, so prayer and praying are crucial to spiritual life and growth.

A breakthrough in the treatment of Down's Syndrome children captured my attention in an article entitled 'Waistcoat of hope for tragic babies!' The wonder waistcoat, developed by the British Institute of Brain Injured

Children in Somerset, when in place forces the child to breathe correctly at regular intervals. With the increase of oxygen to the brain, the whole of the body and its functions is effected. Prolonged treatment can ultimately change the shape of their faces, reforming noses and defining eyes. When children begin breathing correctly through their noses with the aid of the waistcoat, remarkable changes occur. Breathing correctly is natural unless a blockage or malfunction occurs, as in Down's Syndrome.

The same is true of prayer. God made us with a natural capacity to communicate and love him in the relationship that is at the heart of all creation and initiates and effects all other relationships. Adam and Eve walked and talked naturally with God, nothing clouding or spoiling their relationship. Selfishness and sin blew all that apart. Ever since, men and women have searched endlessly for the ideal relationship. Their God-shaped emptiness has been unsuccessfully filled either by cold religion, the occult, materialism or human achievement. They cry out in desperation to an unknown God or worship the gods of this world.

When we accept Jesus into our lives, he heals that dislocated relationship with God. He comes into our daily lives by the power of the Holy Spirit literally to show us the truth about every aspect of life: 'The Holy Spirit will guide you into all truth' (Jn 16:13). He needs to permeate every corner of our lives, with our consent, to change and reshape us. Our desires, motives, hopes, ambitions are all slowly revolutionised. Prayer is that relationship of discovery with the God of creation and communication. As we explore and enter this relationship of prayer, we grow more like Jesus with his capacity to live life to the full. One little girl who had the distinctive features of a Down's Syndrome victim, after using the wonder waistcoat, now looks just like her strapping healthy father.

Workout session

Alone

(1) Every time you pray, start with a simple request for God to teach you to pray. Don't necessarily expect immediate answers; be patient as well as expectant. Ask him for an alert spirit to recognise his answers in refreshing your relationship with him. Enjoy his company.

(2) Obtain a notebook for future notes and consultation. Practise capturing on paper those things God teaches you when praying and reading the Bible.

(3) Write down the methods that help you in prayer. Eg, speaking out loud, or a particular position or place.

(4) In the book of Luke, find out how many times you see Jesus praying and in what kinds of places. With these in mind, explore different places and times for your private prayer. Note down those most effective for you. If a whole book is a marathon for you, try searching just in Luke 9 and 10.

In groups

(1) Share your favourite and least favourite subject at school. Describe the teacher of each of those subjects.

(2) Share some of your helps or hindrances in prayer.

(3) From your individual search, list the places where Jesus prayed and note the practicality of doing the same today. Eg, Luke 5:16, Luke 6:12 and Luke 9:18.

(4) Discuss your most effective place(s) and position(s) for prayer. These don't have to be mentioned in the Bible. Why are they effective for you?

(5) Share any new lesson you have learned as a direct result of praying, 'Lord, teach me to pray.'

Recommended reading

Jim Graham, *Prayer* (SU Publication)
Mike and Katie Morris *Praying Together* (Kingsway: Eastbourne)
Geoff Baker *You Can Grow as a Christian* (SU/Saltmine)

3

Fit to Drop

Ivan Lendl was one of the top male tennis seeds at Wimbledon in 1988. He was almost down and out in his fourth-round match with Australian Mark Woodford. The cold statistics on the umpire's scorecard—7–5, 6–7, 6–7, 7–5, 10–8—only revealed the match score, not the cliff-hanging excitement, the drained emotions, the demands on stamina and the heart-stopping tension created in players and spectators alike. Lendl picked himself off the grass to reveal the fighting qualities of a world champion. After the four hours and forty-six minute marathon fight, Lendl emerged from the massage table saying, 'You are not so much drained physically as mentally, but I think I can rebound from that.'

How well do we rebound from the physical and mental gymnastics of life? How is our survival rate? Are we at a down and almost out stage, or fighting to keep our head above water? Life holds its fair share of ups and downs for all of us. Many of us would admit more of the latter as we spiral into depression or struggle with deteriorating circumstances. We are urged to fight for number one and our instincts react to survive.

With the dawning of the age of fitness, fighting the flab has become fashionable. Sports complexes, community centres, race tracks and swimming pools have filled with all ages subjecting themselves to various programmes of exercises and routines, seeking to tone up and adjust weight. Diet, fashion and cosmetics have been influenced by the wave of interest in the image of health, emphasised in adverts, education and the media.

In the wake of this tidal wave of interest, there is a struggling majority left feeling breathless, shapeless and useless. The fighting goes far deeper than the extra inches and calories, or the thickening waist and double chin. Our fight is against our deeper self-image. We can always find someone else better looking, more capable and successful than ourselves. This causes crippling introspection and an 'all-in' mentality. We feel inadequate, inferior, incapable, insecure, insensitive, inefficient, introvert, incoherent ... in fact, in a mess!

This image of ourselves is so paltry, when the God who made us and wants to indwell us is so mighty. We aggravate all situations when we are out of harmony and struggling with our own identity. Our acceptance of others is determined by our acceptance of ourselves. We fight for position, reputation, fulfilment, satisfaction, security and acceptance. The secret to all these is not found by fighting for them, but by accepting them from the one person who has done all the fighting for us and in fact commands us to 'stop fighting and know that I am God' (Ps 46:10, GNB).

The God of the twenty-first century, unchanged down

through the ages, can be known, not just by cold hard facts, but in a life-changing relationship. We need a new relationship with God. He is not a distant deity pressing buttons to control the world. At the heart of his creation is relationship. His making of mankind was in all ways different from his authoritative ordering of the universe. From explosive commands such as, 'Let there be light', we read, 'And now we will make human beings and they will be like us and resemble us' (Gen 1:26, GNB). Instead of delegating creation to some angel or lesser being, he got down to it himself, entering intimately into his creative work. 'Then the Lord God took some soil from the ground and formed man out of it' (Gen 2:7). Instead of flicking a switch or turning a dial, we read that 'he breathed life-giving breath into his nostrils and the man began to live'.

This is literally breathtaking. God, our Creator, initiated all human life in close relationship. It was he who out of this caring closeness observed the loneliness of man and again provided the perfect answer: 'Then the Lord God made the man fall into a deep sleep, and while he was sleeping he took out one of man's ribs and closed up the flesh. He formed a woman out of the rib and brought her to him' (Gen 2:21). In the next verses we see how relationships all stem from our healthy, primary relationship with God. In chapter 3 of Genesis, disobedience disrupted this perfect plan for successful relationship, and Satan had a field day in the Garden of Eden. In the biggest step of selfishness of all time, man rejected intimacy with God. Death became reality and the fight for survival was on. Ever since, man has been searching for the perfect relationship.

David Cassidy admitted in an interview on television concerning his pop idol image, that he had everything he desired except the perfect relationship for which he was always searching. We yearn for security in our personal life, our family life, business, neighbourhood and church

life. We long to belong, need to be needed, and love to
be loved. We have our invisible drawer of life's labels to
cling to for security and position. Husband, wife, parent,
teacher, secretary, church worker, employee, boss, etc.
God isn't looking for performance, he is looking for
relationship. His search is not for missionaries, singers,
successful businessmen, leaders, elders, deacons, seminar
speakers. His simple request is 'Do you love me? Stop
your fighting for position, status and security, and accept
all of these and more, in a love relationship with me.'

In the heat of the day, alone, tired and gasping with
thirst, Jesus sat talking to a woman who was a failure in
relationships. It was to this broken lady that he revealed
what God was seeking for—true worshippers. God says to
his chosen people in Hosea 6:5–6, 'What I want from you is
plain and clear; I want your constant love, not your animal
sacrifices. I would rather have my people know me than
burn offerings to me.' What God longs to see through all
our strivings for position, reputation and success is purely
and simply a heart after him. We no longer sacrifice like
people did in the Old Testament, but on our twentieth-
century altars we carefully arrange our church going,
positions, witnessing, and our 'grit-your-teeth' routines of
religion and discipline. God sweeps all these aside and
says, 'Stop fighting! Be still and know that I am God.'

It was God's intention for human beings to find their
identity not in self, but in their relationship with him. As
God by his Holy Spirit permeates our whole personality,
he slowly transforms us into the person he intends us to
be. We discover not only what it is to be fully human, but
also to be fully ourselves. Communicating with God
deepens our knowledge of him. The more we know of
God, the clearer we see and accept ourselves, and we are
then released to accept and affirm others.

Changing schools is a big step in every child's life. For
me it was a massive leap, as it plunged me into a

secondary school in London where sport was high on the agenda. I soon made friends with my new classmates, but one was special. Rowena was tall and slender alongside my (then) short frame, and I looked up to her in all ways. We soon found our temperaments and interests were similar and there followed seven years of school life and three years of college, enriched by always having a best friend around. I was never alone; I always had someone to share with or moan with. The disaster of having to repeat a year before important exams because of our substandard work was softened because we did it together. Togetherness is such an important ingredient in life and the hours of cycling to school in all weathers, the team work in competing on the same side in netball matches, the coffee and lunch breaks spent in each other's company, all cemented a relationship that in retrospect has greatly influenced my approach and enjoyment of life and all other relationships.

Then came the cold hard winter of 1962–63. Britain was in the grip of the iciest weather in many years. The countryside was transformed and the normally sun-drenched golf course at Eastbourne became an undulating nursery slope for skiers. Our breath hung crystallised on the air, and I was known for the constant chattering of my teeth as we braved the elements and walked by the stormy sea. Hunched against the cutting wind, you might have asked why a cosy college room wouldn't have been a better option. Why submit oneself to the isolated, bitter surroundings? Here was an escape. A time to be alone with the one person I was hungry to know. After weeks of my study and separation, Doug was on a brief visit from London, and we needed to talk and listen, to laugh and cry, to encourage and comfort. In conversation, in silence, in love. As my friendship with Doug developed, his daily letters to me in my last two terms of college were snatched up, devoured and read so often they were memorised. They lay under my pillow and became extremely tattered with the continual reading. My usually haphazard corresponding became regular and urgent in my answering of his letters, and I counted the minutes in the day to when I would see him again.

These two committed friendships, among others, have had a profound effect on my life. There is an acceptance of me written right across them that helped me develop as a person and as a result revel in the other person's company. That is what God longs for. We see it in his confrontation with the woman at the well in John 4:23, when he says, 'The Father seeks true worshippers.' God longs for a deep committed relationship with his people. An excitement in each other's company, a longing for each other's presence, a kindred spirit. This longing caused him to strip off his greatness, to lay aside his majesty, in order to mix with those he had made on this earth. To walk and talk with them, laugh and cry with them, to live and die for them. Why all this to end in death? In order to reverse that last statement. He died to live for them, to live *in* them and open up a powerful new relationship with them. That's the relationship that starts when we ask Jesus into our lives.

How do we get to know God? By spending every moment possible with him. Talking with him, listening to him, getting to know what is on his heart. As day by day I repeated my request, 'Lord, teach me to pray', I started to see the ridiculous quality of a relationship based on an hour or so, one day a week. A few reluctant, snatched minutes of parrot-fashion prayer. Cries for help, and shallow thank-yous. I became more aware of how God felt in this relationship. This letter, by an anonymous writer, captures a fraction of the ache in God's heart.

Dear Friend
How are you? I just had to send a note to tell you how much I care for you. I saw you yesterday as you were talking with your friends. I waited all day hoping you would want to talk

with me too. I gave you a sunset to close your day and a cool breeze to rest you . . . and I waited. You never came. It hurt me. But I still love you because I am your friend.

I saw you sleeping last night and longed to touch your brow, so I spilled moonlight upon your face. Again I waited, wanting to rush down so we could talk. I have so many gifts for you. You awoke and rushed off to work. My tears were in the rain.

If you would only listen to me! I love you. I tried to tell you in blue skies, and in the quiet green grass. I whisper it in leaves on the trees and breathe it in the colour of the flowers. I shout it to you in mountain streams, give the birds love songs to sing. I clothe you with warm sunshine and perfume the air with nature's scents.

My love for you is deeper than the ocean and bigger than the biggest need in your heart.

Ask me! Talk with me! Please don't forget me. I have so much to share with you.

I won't hassle you any further. It is your decision. I have chosen you and I still wait—because I love you.
Your friend

Jesus.

On reading this letter, I imagined the effect on Doug if I barged in to him first thing in the morning in full flight saying, 'Dear Doug, can't be long, give me my week's allowance of money. More if possible. Clear up the mess I've made, look after the kids. Sorry about what I said last night, there was something else, but I've forgotten. Can't stop! Maybe see you sometime. I will try to remember to talk to you. Sue.' Add to this, weeks of silence and pre-occupation and our relationship would have died rapidly.

I began to discover that I did not naturally want to spend time with God. Sin had destroyed that desire, and part of the Spirit's work in me to guide me into the truth about life was to replace that desire. He raised within me new requests. Following my 'Lord, teach me to pray' came, 'Give me a real hunger for your presence. Give me a longing to be with you, to read your word and hear your voice.' I stopped gritting my teeth to follow a rule and regulation, and started to enjoy a relationship and a friendship.

This new experience of true friendship and true worship is totally dependent on God's initiation. He raises the expectancy in my heart and the longing to deepen our relationship, and I constantly need to ask him for his awakening. In all relationships, familiarity can breed contempt—and contempt is a product of our old nature. The answer to deterioration in relationships is spiritfulness. In Ephesians 3:19 we read about being 'filled with the very nature of God!' God fills us with his ability to have successful relationships.

God started to nudge me into an awareness of his continual presence. At the most unexpected moments I became conscious of him travelling with me in the car, walking through busy market places, shopping, ironing, gardening, walking, talking, eating. His presence was real, almost tangible. I started sharing with him, at first hesitantly, sometimes in my mind, at other times when alone out loud. This literally opened my eyes to a whole new experience of prayer at any time and anywhere.

After several walks by the sea, appreciating the surroundings with God and telling him so, I experienced a frustration of stopping in full verbal flight when I passed others enjoying the seashore. Fear of embarrassment interrupted my conversation with God. Sharing my open-air experience with someone else led to relaxed walks with a friend when conversation became prayer and prayer became conversation. Sometimes in companionable silence, other times in verbal conversation, we walked and talked with God. There were no embarrassed pauses as we passed others, they were unaware of our third companion. They observed natural lively conversation. As our bodies were refreshed physically, so God refreshed our minds and spirits through the exercise of prayer.

What a discovery to find that instead of ruining my concentration, praying with my eyes open heightened my awareness of God as I saw him in the ordinary everyday things of life. This exercise revolutionised long car journeys as I was able to share in depth with God and use those otherwise wasted hours. Praise tapes are a modern gift to travellers, lifting us out of the frustration of traffic jams into the presence of God. Motorway monotony is transformed into a companionable consultation with the one who knows all about the way ahead and longs to prepare us for it. We can learn to listen to God too through the many tapes of leading Bible teachers and also God's spoken word from the Bible on tape. Walking the dog, driving to work, cycling to school, pacing the golf course, or walking the fells in the Lake District, all these can be opportunities for time with our God.

Workout session

Alone

(1) Write a letter to God in answer to the one in this chapter written to you.

(2) Recollect some human relationships which have helped or hindered your image and your relationship with God. Eg, a parent or friend.

(3) Remind yourself of God's presence with you wherever you are. Eg, ask his help in short cuts and

saving in shopping! Discuss with him appointments or decisions you make at work.

(4) Write down an 'all-in' experience you've had recently—and if just writing things down makes you feel 'all-in', *tell* God about it. Now apply Psalm 46:10 to that situation and feeling: 'Stop fighting. Be still and know that I am God.' Accept God's unconditional love and then accept yourself as you are for God to work in you.

In groups

(1) Don't let's limit our prayer to a slot of formality at the end of our time as a group—let our conversation be with God. Remember that God is among you, and your discussion and sharing can be a practical presentation of yourselves as you really are to God in prayer.

(2) In pairs or in groups, write something positive you see in your partner or others. Share them together.

(3) Admit an inadequacy about self-image or share a humorous occasion when you were made to feel small. Learn to laugh at yourself with others.

(4) Pray together and for each other, asking for God's adequacy to fill our inadequacy. Be specific—eg, ask for God's confidence to replace your shyness and lack of confidence. Remember vagueness cripples our prayers.

(5) Explore the possibility of walking and talking together about these exercises and include short times of prayer on these walks. Awkwardness and embarrassment will soon disappear the more you practice this very real and literal walk with God.

Recommended reading

Pete Meadows *Pressure Points* (Kingsway: Eastbourne)

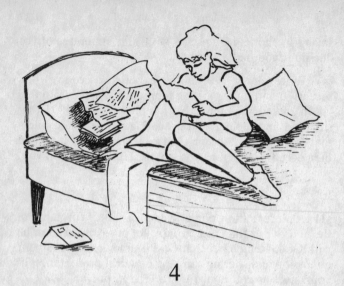

4

Love Letters Straight from the Heart

The communication between Doug and me in those romantic days at college was not only based on surprise visits or spur of the moment rendezvous. There is a danger in a relationship which is all spontaneity without the balance of careful planning and thoughtful structure. Neither of us would have known where we stood, and our security would have been shaky. Our knowledge and love of one another grew more from our regular letter writing and a phone call once a week. I was first down to the student common room each morning, scanning the post for my letter. No one could get a word in as I hung on to every sentence and reread the treasured words, taking them with me into the hectic days of lectures and training. Towards noon, over a snatched lunch, I would sit down and answer that letter, eager to share how I felt about the things he had written and telling the many little details of my day. What a shame many of us give up the communication of writing when we are in each other's company more often. Far more is left to the imagination, and that so often leads to misunderstanding. It is essential, where possible, in all relationships to write to each other so misunderstandings don't magnify and hurts are healed. So why did I not discover this in my relationship with God? Was it because I did not ask him to teach me to pray?

It was 3.00am on a cold April morning. I had been running a temperature for days, and groped my way downstairs for a hot drink. I was feeling low physically and as sleep seemed elusive, I started to write down those things that were concerning me and the jobs I needed to get on with the next day. That scrap of insignificant paper turned out to be the first page of what has now become a multi-volume dialogue with God. When concentration is difficult, which is frequent with me, the discipline of capturing my thoughts on paper directs my praying and exercises my mind. I can lay my prayers before the Lord and get concerns and problems out of my system and onto paper. What was at first a spiritual exercise has also proved to be an effective mental and psychological exercise. As I struggled through that first letter to God, I found I had been writing for an hour! In those days I would never have kept my concentration for that length of time. Over the past years, writing my prayers has helped me know and understand God and myself.

I had kept a rather tatty prayer diary in an endeavour to keep me praying regularly for people and situations. It was on a weekly basis and I shared family and friends' needs and joys across the pages in formal note form, trying to remember to record the answers when possible. Our church has a similar method whereby all the members of the church are prayed for throughout the week. Unlike the diary, my dialogue was living communication. It gave permanence to daily occurrences and lessons which would otherwise have been lost in time and the 'hectivity' of life. It gave perspective to my growing relationship with God, and released tensions which would have been left as wordless, buried frustrations. It demanded a growing honesty that enabled me to face up to the real me and come to terms with situations. The more I accept myself, the more I am able to address outside issues and the concerns of others. I slowly discovered through my growing need to write, that I am a very lazy thinker and communicator. I leave sentences in mid air, and rarely pursue my thoughts to their conclusion. In conversation I persistently escape into phrases such as 'you know', and 'you see what I mean?'. I leave to my facial expression and the hearer's imagination my opinions, hopes and observations. If the truth were known, in most cases the listener doesn't know, cannot see what I mean, or has a distorted view of my ramblings. Writing literally clarifies how we really feel. It unscrambles our knotted emotions and releases our trapped inner selves.

An extreme example of this was found in a hospital locker after an old lady had died. She couldn't speak, and was only occasionally seen writing.

LOOK CLOSER—by Phyllis McCormack

What do you see, nurses, what do you see?
Are you thinking when you are looking at me,
A crabbit old woman not very wise,
Uncertain of habit with far away eyes,
Who dribbles her food and makes no reply,

When you say in a loud voice, 'I do wish you'd try,'
Who seems not to notice the things that you do,
And forever is losing a stocking or shoe,
Who unresisting or not let you do as you will,
With bathing and feeding the long day to fill,
Is that what you are thinking, is that what you see?
Then open your eyes nurse, you're not looking at me.
I'll tell you who I am as I sit here so still,
As I move at your bidding as I eat at your will,
I'm a small child of ten with a father and mother,
Brothers and sisters who love one another,
A young girl of sixteen with wings on her feet,
Dreaming that soon a lover she'll meet;
A bride now at twenty—my heart gives a leap,
Remembering the vows that I promised to keep;
At twenty-five now I have young of my own,
Who need me to build a secure, happy home;
A young woman of thirty, my young now grow fast,
Bound to each other with ties that should last;
At forty my young sons will soon all be gone,
But my man stays beside me to see I don't mourn;
At fifty once more babies play round my knee,
Again we know children my loved one and me.
Dark days are upon me, my husband is dead,
I look at the future I shudder with dread,
For my young are all busy rearing young of their own
And I think of the years and the love I have known.
I'm an old woman now and nature is cruel,
'Tis her jest to make old age look like a fool.
The body it crumbles, grace and vigour depart,
There now is a stone where I once had a heart.
But inside this old carcase a young girl still dwells
And now and again my battered heart swells.
I remember the joys, I remember the pain
And I am laughing and living life over again.

I think of the years all too few—gone too fast,
And accept the stark fact that nothing can last.
So open your eyes nurses, open and see,
Not a crabbit old woman, look closer ... SEE ME.

This old lady had come to terms with the 'real me' in a powerful way as she sat helpless, dependent on others, and seemingly uncommunicative. The sadness is that in those last few words, 'nothing can last', she doesn't seem to have discovered the one thing that is lasting and can transform the frailty and transience of human life. That is our relationship with God. This is the one fact and experience of life that improves with age and is perfected beyond death. Anything that improves my understanding of that incredible relationship is worth exploring, and capturing my thoughts on paper has helped sharpen my focus on God.

In my early days of exploring this language of prayer, I constantly struggled to find the right words. I found the expression of others accurately described my wordless longings. The Bible is a perfect example. We may experience the excitement of a promise God has given us, and long to express it as did Mary. When Elizabeth says to her, 'Blessed is he who has believed that what the Lord has said to her will be accomplished!' (Lk 1:45), Mary responds with the words familiar to most of us as the Magnificat, 'My soul glorifies the Lord and my spirit rejoices in God my Saviour, for he has been mindful of the humble state of his servant. From now on, all generations will call me blessed, for the Mighty One has done great things for me—Holy is his name' (Lk 1:46–55).

Such a burst of excitement is also captured in 1 Samuel chapter 2 verses 1–10: 'My heart rejoices in the Lord; in the Lord my horn is lifted high. My mouth boasts over my enemies, for I delight in your deliverance. There is no-one holy like the Lord, there is no-one besides you; there is no Rock like our God.' Both women are bubbling over to God in love, because of the miracle of new life within their inadequate and unworthy bodies. Mary, an ordinary teenager, was to give birth to Jesus.

Hannah, after years of infertility, produced Samuel—a gift of God. Who wouldn't shout 'hurray'? As I wrote out for myself these words, reread them and made them my own, the wonder of the new life born in me by the Holy Spirit hit me with renewed amazement. My relationship with God is a miracle.

What about the times of desolation when we pour out our agonised thoughts in a kaleidoscope of hurt confusion. The first chapter of my last book *Fit for a King* was one such explosion of feeling. Returning at 2.00am from the death-bed of a friend, through whom I had learned so much, caused a mass of bewildered questions. As I trapped the tumbling thoughts on paper, the one clear phrase on that first night of writing was, 'We live in a world so aware of the physical body—we exercise it, we feed it, we pamper it, we clothe it, we sauna it, we paint it, we measure it, we weigh it, we massage it, we tan it, we exploit it, we sell it, and then eventually we leave it!' Little else made sense. This experience and the recording of it among many other lessons enlarged my awareness and understanding of our world and its needs. I will often turn back to that dark night of bereavement when asking God for a burden for those around me who don't yet know the power of God's life in theirs.

What about those times when our communication is hampered by a cloud of concern for those we love so much? A prayer wrung from the heart of Amy Carmichael lay my thoughts naked before God, not only for my offspring but for the future generation of our church, country and world.

> Father hear me, I am praying,
> Hear the words my heart is saying,
> I am praying for my children.
> Keep them from the powers of evil

From the secret hidden peril,
From the whirlpool that would suck them,
From the treacherous quicksand pluck them,
From the wordling's hollow gladness,
From the sting of faithless sadness.
Holy Father, save my children.
Through life's troubled waters steer them,
Through life's bitter battle cheer them,
Father, Father! Be thou near them.
Read the language of my longing,
Read the wordless pleadings thronging,
Holy Father for my children,
And where'er they may abide,
Bring them home at eventide.

'Hear the language of my longing, hear the wordless pleadings thronging.' I can apply these words to so many situations. Through the developing exercise of writing, God who created us to communicate and is expert in the art, loves to unlock the hidden recesses of our heart. He identifies our needs and longings and gives us his perspective on human life and need. We can pray far more intelligently right to the heart of the situation instead of skating clumsily around on the surface. Prayer and worship is an affair of the heart. Although it involves outward acts, it is an inward attitude and God loves to hear our expressions of love, however hesitant: 'I love you Lord and I lift my voice, to worship you O my soul rejoice. Take joy my King in what you hear, let it be a sweet, sweet sound in your ear.'

When Stephen and Duncan, our sons, were first learning to talk, never once did Doug or I tell them to go away until they could talk correctly. One of the most moving memories I have is when one of them wrapped his sticky fingers around my face and whispered, 'I lub you, Mum!' The more we talk to God, whether in speech, writing, singing, thinking or through the language of living, our communication will improve.

One bright spring day back in 1963, I woke with my usual excitement and expectancy. Doug's daily letters, since the Christmas of our first commitment in relationship, had transformed my morning routine. As I hurtled down the stairs, pulling on my tracksuit in full flight, I screeched to a halt by the post table, scanning it for his distinctive, bold handwriting.

No letter! No Doug! My heart sank. I had become dependent on those daily words of fun, encouragement, concern and love. The teasing came thick and fast from fellow students and I had to hide my disappointment to survive that strangely dark day. My pen dragged over the paper as I wrote to Doug. No questions to answer, no up-to-date news to respond to, no words of comfort and love. That day of disappointment was soon forgotten when next morning I collected two bulging envelopes from the postman. 'Must have been delayed, love,' he said with a wink.

There is no delay with God's letter to us. The Bible is up to date and punctual for each one of us. It tells us in so many ways that God loves us and reveals the secret of living life to the full in close relationship with him. God does not only give us practical principles for life, but also particular plans for each day. Directions, warnings, encouragements and corrections are all found in Scripture for our personal daily lives. To ignore them is to miss what really matters. 'All Scripture is God breathed and is useful for teaching, rebuking, correcting and training in righteousness, so that the man of God may be thoroughly equipped for every good work' (2 Tim 3:16–17).

As I asked God to give me a hunger for his word, he reminded me of those letters I carefully collected each morning and read so often. I asked him to give me an eagerness for his word that would eclipse those love letters of 1963. His love for me is greater than any we experience on this earth: 'Greater love has no-one than this, that one lay down his life for his friends' (Jn 15:13). The secret to this crucial relationship lies in the words that follow in verse 14: 'You are my friends if you do what I command!' The Bible is packed with reasonable guidelines for our protection and wellbeing. As we approach the twenty-first century, it is becoming glaringly obvious that what God says makes sense. Relevant subjects including homosexuality, war, peace, women's equality, love and hate, the occult and mediums are all dealt with clearly and precisely in the Bible. God's presence and his word are vital to successful living. There are many books to guide us in our study of God's word, and I list some of them at the end of the chapter. It is, however, so refreshing at some time during the day or week to pick up the Bible as a love letter, remembering that every word is written with the love that died for you. Try starting with the book of James in the New Testament. This is easy to read as a letter, because it literally is one, containing practical wisdom for the nitty gritty of everyday life. Remember, as we read the Bible we are giving God the opportunity to speak to us, either through a verse, a thought or later on applying it to an event in our day. Watch out! Our God's about!

Workout session

Alone

(1) Read James 1 and note verse 22: 'Do not merely listen to the word and so deceive yourselves. Do what it says.' Compare this with John 15:14—'You are my friends if you do what I command.' Which verse in James 1 are you not only going to listen to, but do something about? Note it down in your book, and also note your plan of action. Be specific and ask God's help and wisdom in the action. (Verse 5!)

(2) Explore writing to God. Remember we are all different and our relationships with God are unique. What works in one relationship doesn't necessarily work in another, but if we don't try, we will never know.

(3) Memorise Psalm 119. Don't panic! Note verse 11: 'I have hidden your word in my heart that I might not sin against you.' Take your time, but remember, actors learn a lot more lines than these!

(4) Get out and walk, cycle or drive and talk with God. Allow God to speak to you through his creation or through the hustle and bustle of everyday life.

Group activity or in pairs

(1) Share your verse from James and plan of action. Discuss your successes and failures in obedience.

(2) Using the verse through which God spoke to you, write down a one-sentence prayer. For example, 'Please Lord, give me wisdom in the interview that I have on Monday.' Note James 1:5.

(3) Compare Psalm 119 verse 11—'I have hidden your word in my heart that I might not sin against you'—with James 1 verse 21b—'And humbly accept the word planted in you, which can save you.' Discuss how we can hide God's word in our heart and allow him to plant it there.

Recommended reading

Edward England, *Keeping a Spiritual Journal* (Highland Books: Crowborough)
Daily Walk Bible (Tyndale House Publishers)
Dave Pope, *You Can Discover God's Will* (SU/Saltmine)

5

Don't Panic!

Don't push! Please don't push! The agonised cry of the midwife cut across the bedroom where little Alison Page was about to be born. My mother, a trained nurse and midwife, was also encouraging my sister to hold on. Tears crept silently down her cheeks as she remembered her stillborn daughter born twenty years before. Was history going to repeat itself?

All had run so smoothly with Mum arriving, as she always did, just as she was needed. The baby was due at any time and a good brisk walk was suggested to Becky Falls, the Devonian beauty spot. Dartmoor was bathed in summer sunshine and before the walk was completed Helen, my sister, was bathed in perspiration—labour had begun!

As Dartmoor's animals and birds slept peacefully that

night, Helen literally laboured through the dark hours, her mind set on the long-awaited daughter and granddaughter our whole family of sons hoped for! As Alison made her appearance, her little blue face caused the midwife's sharp order. The umbilical cord was too short and was wrapped tightly round the little one's neck. What had been an incredible lifeline of nourishment and oxygen for the past nine months, now became a deadly tourniquet cutting off the oxygen supply. Twenty years before, this had proved fatal to my little sister. Now, skilled hands fought to free the baby. The cord was cut and Alison entered this world. 'We've got our little girl!' Helen cried to her husband David, and the family welcomed the first granddaughter with a sigh of relief.

It was not until several years later that my sister realised the long-term results of that tough delivery. Alison was deaf. One day as a strapping toddler, she was listening to her bedtime story, her intent eyes never leaving my sister's face. Finally, closing the book, Helen kissed her goodnight and stood to leave the room. Flicking the switch, she called her final goodnight to be answered with words that have stayed with her to this day: 'Switch the light on Mummy, I can't hear you!' Conveyed to the specialist, Alison's request confirmed a fear that had grown over the months. The vital supply of oxygen had been severely cut down at birth, and had affected the area of the brain that controlled hearing. Without aid, Alison was severely handicapped.

That cry in the darkness from a little child perfectly describes how I felt in the early days when developing the two-way relationship of prayer. 'Switch the light on God, I can't hear you!' How I longed to see and hear him so that there was no doubt what he wanted to say. I understood with renewed force the handicap I had inherited. Cut off from God, the true source of spiritual life, I was spiritually deaf, dumb and blind to God's presence and his provision. In my healed relationship with him, he was developing within me that ability to hear his voice once more—a whole new experience that takes time. Alison's need was heightened as her mum turned from her and switched the light off. Her eyes were used to being fixed on her mum's face as she saw the words shaped on her lips. Do you sometimes feel God has literally turned from you and no longer has time or words for you? You are not alone! In Psalm 10 we see a cry from the Psalmist's heart: 'Why O Lord do you stand far off? Why do you hide yourself in times of trouble?' Then in Psalm 22 verse 1 David uses the agonised words that Jesus used himself on the cross: 'My God, my God, why have you forsaken me? Why are you so far from saving me?'

We have grown accustomed to the horrific pictures on our television screens showing the results of famine. Yet none of these compare with the silent impact of the prophetic pictures of Amos 8:11–12—'The days are coming, declares the Sovereign Lord, when I will send a famine through the land . . . not a famine of food or a thirst for water, but a famine of hearing the words of the Lord. Men will stagger from sea to sea and wander from North to East, searching for the word of the Lord, but they will not find it.' The days have come, down through the years, and particularly in this century, when a famine of hearing God's voice has caused havoc. Not only has the world felt it in its wild search for satisfaction and purpose, but the church has been rendered ineffective, with no voice to the nation. The desire to hear God's voice and to wait and listen in his presence has diminished. In the last three decades we have seen a move of God that has revolutionised Christian lives, churches and worship. As the Holy Spirit has swept through the country he has dealt individually and collectively with thousands—of whom I was one. Slowly but firmly, God breathed fresh life into a cold pattern of Christian observances, revealing himself as a passionate God of close relationship, but also of utter holiness. It was this confrontation which I remember by the insatiable hunger which he gave me in my urgent request, 'Lord, teach me to pray.' In this progressive, personal and practical instruction, I now came to the exciting area of listening to and hearing God. I repeatedly felt I was at the foot of a great mountain of discovery, unsure of the route and feeling very insignificant alongside the awesome knowledge that God could actually speak to me.

Talking of mountains draws me irresistibly back to those ski slopes. It was the last day of our holiday in the French Alps. I climbed out of the lift for my last taste of the mountain air. A few swift runs down the slopes would be imprinted on my memory for the return to the exhaust-fumed cities of Britain. Being lunchtime the slopes were almost deserted save a father and his tiny son. It was obviously the three-year-old's first experience of skiing when, all helmet, skis and dummy, he clung whimpering to the button lift. With a sharp lurch of the ski lift the little one was suddenly catapulted off his perch into the soft snow where he buried his helmeted head into the damp mittens. His whimpers turned into yells. As I twisted awkwardly to see this crumpled heap of scrawling humanity, his big six-foot dad came to the rescue. His reassuring remarks were completely drowned out by the little mite's yells. Eventually the dad knelt in front of him, took the little head in his hands, and firmly raising his face until eyeball to eyeball he said, 'Come on son, Dad's here, we will both go up together!' The little lad's face was a transformed picture.

In exploring this whole area of hearing God's voice, we are not alone. We have a God who speaks in many varied ways, and he says to you and me, 'Come on son (or daughter), Daddy's here, we'll go up together.' I very often miss his reassuring presence and words of encouragement, because my demanding yells drown out that still small voice. God comes just where we are—in the office, at the kitchen sink, at dawn through to dusk, wherever we are, at whatever hour, he is a God who communicates with his people. He longs to lift us out of our huddle of selfish whimpers for help to train us in the art of listening, hearing and obeying.

How can he heal our handicap of spiritual deafness? How can he bring to an end our personal famine of hearing his voice? What hinders our hearing? First, one of the biggest hindrances is the pace of life. As the years accelerate towards the twenty-first century, we are swept along in the avalanche of progress at an alarming rate. Our labour-saving devices, time management awareness and filofax mentality can all lead to days where every minute is accounted for and prioritised. As a result, we cannot cope with stillness and inactivity and find it difficult to listen to any voice which interrupts our routine, let alone God who demands our attention to be still continually and know him. No wonder his voice is silent to us and his presence seems far off.

As I was writing these words, overlooking my garden, a minor explosion at the other end of the room shot me out of my seat. A sparrow swooping down from the freedom of the sky overshot the pile of crumbs on our patio and flew through the open door to circle round and out towards the trees. The only problem was, what seemed to be a clear route back to freedom was strangely blocked by a transparent obstacle—glass. There followed a crazed circling of the room with a continual beating of wings against windows and doors. It wasn't until that frenzied bundle of feathers had worn itself out that it came to rest long enough for me to guide its beaten little body through an open window.

How long is it since we came to rest long enough for

God to lead us into his greater freedom, out of our confines of striving and organisation? Is God our pacemaker or are we speeding on without him, swooping into the danger of a trapped existence filled with obstacles? We can often see the beauty and freedom beyond our human confines, but it only mocks us as we circle in a continual round of stifled activity, straining to be free but knocking ourselves out in the search for release.

In all walks of life, from the troubleshooting executive to the retired senior citizen, our fast-moving society affects us. We have to prove our performance and excuse any relaxation as almost a crime. God who made us active and with the need to organise and plan says, 'Be still, stop fighting, and know that I am God' (Ps 46:10). In order to be more effectively active we must first learn to be still and listen to God. We need to acquire a stillness and a listening spirit that will permeate all our actions, even in our most hectic times. Although it is important to have times of bodily stillness and relaxation, the command 'Be still!' in Psalm 46 in the Hebrew is more like the sharp command 'Enough! Listen to me!' which needs a quietness and obedience of mind and spirit which will keep us listening right through our days' activities.

How do we cultivate this quietness of spirit and peace of mind? It is interesting to see that the legacy left to the disciples by Jesus himself when he left the earth in bodily form, was '*peace*'. Jesus had nothing of earthly value to give them, but the most sought after gift down through all time is peace, and in John 14:27 he tells them of their inheritance. 'Peace I leave with you; my peace I give you. I do not give to you as the world gives. Do not let your hearts be troubled and do not be afraid.' After his death he appears to the disciples, a risen miracle, and reminds them again of the incredible gift that is theirs. 'Peace be with you. ... Why are you troubled and why do doubts rise in your minds? Look at my hands and my feet. It is I myself! Touch me and see' (Lk 24:36–39). This is no airy-fairy feeling; this is a concrete, workable peace. As Jesus draws their attention to his hands and feet, they see the torn nailprints. This was a peace that had survived the most extreme pressure and pain any-one can bear. Peace that is powerful—peace that was theirs, and peace that is ours. A peace that persists through rejection, wrong accusation, misunderstanding, disap-pointment, misrepresentation and isolation. A peace that reaches every shattered nerve and bereaved heart, soothes each hurt emotion and wounded spirit, and refreshes the over crowded, racing mind, enabling it to discern the priorities of God from the ambitions of self.

How can I practise this peace in a life that is bombarded from all sides with confusion, fear and pressure of all description? First, by admitting that I can never achieve this peace and stillness myself. It is not something manufactured or negotiated by man; it is simply a gift from God to be accepted within a close relationship with him. Our source of peace is not dependent on circum-stances or friends which vary and come and go. Our lifeline is God himself. We must draw continually from his inexhaustible supply.

After an hour of exercise in our keep fit group, we are all longing for the few minutes of relaxation necessary to wind down. An important part of resting is breathing; the deep inhaling and exhaling of air steadies the heart-beat, calms the nerves and, if left long enough, encourages a soothing sleep. In anxiety, fear and extreme activity, our breathing becomes rapid and shallow, and will often be held back altogether. I have long discovered that in all situations of crisis, to stop and think and exercise a pattern of deep breathing prevents panic and defuses tension. Through this very necessary bodily exercise I have found an effective spiritual exercise. Seated comfortably, I inhale deeply, slowly lifting my head back as far as it will go. Then I exhale, allowing my head to come forward slowly until my chin nearly rests on my chest. I do this for several minutes as I tell God about those things that are destroying my peace. Here is a guideline I use which obviously varies with circumstances. 'Lord, I exhale my crippling concern for my children, I inhale your ability to take care of them. Lord I exhale my fear for my interview, I inhale your calming of my nerves. Lord, I exhale my loneliness, I inhale your peaceful presence.' Sometimes I exercise in silence and alone, at others times with quiet music and in company. Because of the simplicity of this exercise it can be used at any time with just the basic breathing and without the head action. Just before that important interview, during exams, in confrontation, crisis or accident, we can practise God's peace and bring his calming influence into our situation. As God clears the clutter that causes spiritual deafness, he speaks in direction, comfort and rebuke. Our pace of life is controlled by the peace of the Lord. 'Be still and know that I am God!' (Ps 46:10).

Workout session

Alone

(1) Practise the above exercise and adjust physically and spiritually to personal requirements and requests.

(2) Use the breathing exercise at different times through the day or night. Eg, when you can't sleep and your mind is overactive; in an unexpected crisis.

(3) Memorise Isaiah 26:3—'You will keep in perfect peace him whose mind is steadfast, because he trusts in you.'

When your mind becomes confused or fearful, quote these words and accept the promise.

(4) List times when you feel God is not there. Eg, when he doesn't answer a prayer the way you expected.

Group activity

(1) Have a few fun exercises with a popular choice of music. Finish with your deep breathing, set to a peaceful song of worship.

(2) Share tensions or problems that hinder your peace of mind and prevent you hearing God.

(3) Discuss ways of practising peace in all daily situations.

Recommended reading

Joyce Huggett *Listening to God* (Hodder and Stoughton: London)

6

'You Haven't Heard a Word I've Said!'

Alison Page was just seven years old when she received her new pair of ears, thanks to the Newton Abbot Lions Club. Her multi-freckled face beamed as comedian Don McClean quipped, 'Have you been sunbathing under a tea strainer?' Surrounded by her classmates at Bovey Tracey Primary School, he presented her with a special phonic ear. In 1978 the £800 device consisted of a radio transmitter worn by Alison's teacher, and a radio receiver worn by Alison. This brilliant hearing aid enabled Alison to switch off from environmental sound, but not from her teacher's voice which came from the equivalent of six inches away.

As we deliberately turn from the distractions of life

and face our living God, he promises that he will come far closer than any hearing aid can bring a voice: 'Come near to God and he will come near to you' (Jas 4:8).

It is not only the pace of life that switches off God's living voice, there is also our preoccupation with number one. Television commercials, magazine adverts, leisure activities and education are all obsessed with self-preoccupation, preservation, promotion and improvement. This whole approach to life promotes dependence on God as a weakness, yet such dependence is in fact the only way that number one can be strong: 'I can do everything through Christ who gives me strength' (Phil 4:13). Our relationship with God is a strong, intensely practical faith, not a feeble crutch. It toughens us up for everything that life throws at us. However, in developing our gift of listening to and hearing God, we struggle with our natural inward perspective. Every time I approach God to listen to him, my mind is attacked with all the mundane preoccupations of me, my and mine. In the early days I very nearly gave up the whole idea of listening, because my concentration is so bad and my thoughts were riddled with self. Then God showed me an exercise which, if done regularly like physical exercise, sheds the surplus fat of self-indulgence and sharpens the concentration on God. Equipped with a notebook and pencil, I noted down briefly those selfish distractions as they fought for my attention. Many of them were necessary reminders of a busy family and work life.

(1) Agenda for meeting
(2) Mail to be posted
(3) Meal preparation
(4) Sermon preparation
(5) Hair-cut
(6) Phone parents
(7) Buy present.

As I noted them down, I literally pushed them to one side. As the list got longer the distractions diminished and I struggled through a forest of self-preoccupation to the very presence of God, all else pushed aside.

We have such a practical God, for nothing is wasted in time spent with him. Our list of negative obstacles preventing us from approaching God becomes a plan of positive action for the day, motivated by God's presence and perspective. There are letters to be written, apologies to be made, appointments secured and talks and meals to be prepared. No little item that concerns us is too insignificant for God to attend to. Our self-preoccupation becomes God's occupation. Fresh emphasis is put on the 'I' of 'Be still and know that I am God'.

God is number one, not self! The pattern of modern society is to strive for self, to save time, looks, money and position. As we invest solely in gadgets, exercise routines, plastic surgery, stocks and shares and self-promotion, we lose the whole purpose and heart of life. Self destroys relationships and peace of mind, and by demoting and trivialising God, destroys eternal security. We save all that is transient and temporary and discard all that is permanent and of lasting value. God cuts right across this modern mind set with revolutionary directness: 'Do not conform any longer to the pattern of this world, but be transformed by the renewing of your mind. Then, you will be able to test and approve what God's will is—his good, pleasing and perfect will' (Rom 12:2).

God's will for our lives is neither boring nor unfulfilling; it is the only route which enables us to reach our full potential, physically, mentally, spiritually and socially. Through God's transformation programme, our careers, relationships, recreations, hopes and desires are all affected. Sometimes with spectacular immediacy, more often through a slower, powerful process. It is often in retrospect that we see the miracle of God's moulding of our minds, but this should never prevent us from experiencing and expecting some instant signs of change.

A change in my thinking started surprisingly, and very practically, when watching the news on the television. The catalogue of disasters was spilling out into our lounge, and spectacular interviews were being made to accentuate the dire state of our country and its people. The sighs of frustration and desperation were more than usual, and I became aware of the direction of my comments. 'How will that affect me?' 'We can't walk out freely any more.' 'What about the women?' 'Where does that leave me?' 'I don't like this!'

My whole reaction was self-centred, and because of the spectacular media presentation where good news is no news and sex, violence and catty politics are magnified, I was spiralling into my nightly pool of selfish negativism. 'Do not conform ... be transformed by the renewing of your mind!' Who does the transforming and renewing? The great and mighty God who is in full possession of all the facts of world affairs that reporters try desperately to scoop. He sees behind the wheeling and dealing, he feels the agony of the abused, and he hears the cry of the starved. His perspective, knowledge and timing are perfect, and the renewing of our minds can literally transform our viewing of the news and our vision of the world. The news can become a regular daily prayer time for current affairs.

With God's creative presence and transforming power, he can sharpen our vision, filter out media bias and lift us from destructive negativism to pray positively behind the scenes and into the heart of situations worldwide. We can pray specifically for politicians, pop stars, university students and ambulance staff, as they briefly occupy our living room. The same approach can alter an ordinary newspaper into a living conversation with the one who sees through all the distorted reporting and gives the gift of discernment, which is a spiritual gift with practical application. Prayer is a powerful weapon that can transform our anxious introspection into confident global warfare against evil.

Just as God is in the business of transforming and renewing, so Satan continues his course of wrack and ruin. He delights to capture our human love and concern, to distort it with anxiety and cripple it by bitterness. Where those nearest and dearest to us are concerned, we hurt deeply and insecurity can drive us further into ourselves.

Take the first day at school for our children. The clothes, satchel and lunch are all set out at crack of dawn. After a sleepless night of imagining all possible upsets, we arrive at the school gate. Whether our little one resolutely marches in without a backward glance, or screams and yells her protest, we return home with sinking heart and tear-stinging eyes. This state of vulnerability isn't only a mother's weakness. I can remember Doug accompanying Stephen at the age of eleven to his new secondary school, while I delivered Duncan to his new primary school. Just weeks before, the Barnett family had moved from London to the South coast leaving all our friends behind. As I brewed a fresh cup of tea on my return from that school, I shall always remember Doug's stricken face as he related his longing to say to Stephen, 'Let's forget it, son! You don't have to go to school. Let's go home.' It took us weeks of adjustment, talking and tears before both boys settled in their new home, neighbourhood, church and schools. Little did they know, it took us much longer. In this time of acute inward looking, I remember exaggerating the words that teachers had said to the boys, reported by our sons after tiring days of insecurities. An innocent remark or look became distorted by our vulnerability and introspection.

Preoccupation with self, encouraged by Satan, suffocates our spiritual lives, and our anxiety and emotional stress stifles God's voice in these draining situations. My concern only aggravated the situation by my selfish efforts to make everything right.

The renewing of our minds is so refreshing and creative. Not only does God give us brand-new thought patterns, he also takes the old consuming concern that so often leads to negativism, and transforms it for his positive purposes. Interfering becomes interceding. Whether we are a boss concerned for our company, or a parent concerned for our child, the selfish method swings into action to defend or rectify, and very often confuses and complicates. The issue or situation weighs on our mind and personality clashes magnify in our hearts. 'We take captive every thought to make it obedient to Christ' (2 Cor 10:5b).

As we capture the turmoil of our thoughts, hopes and fears and give them to God, he can turn our consuming concern into prayerful obedience. It is the difference between a body swollen by a deadly malignant growth, and a body swollen by the fresh new growth of a coming baby. The first is destructive and deadly, the second creative and full of life. As God transforms our natural burdens in life, we shed the destructive grip of sin and Satan to corrupt our concern and welcome the expectant labour of intercessory prayer which works together with God for his answer to specific needs and fulfilment of his plans, not ours.

Paul knew the agony of spiritual childbirth, expressed in his descriptive burst of concern to the Galatians: 'My dear children, for whom I am again in the pains of childbirth until Christ is formed in you.' To have a heart for intercession is actually to carry within your body the needs and concerns of others. It is a deep-rooted, fervent longing presented to God. I find it extremely difficult to be fervent while sitting still with my eyes closed.

Personally I can more easily express to God my urgent pleas as I stride around my children's school, saturating the classrooms, pupils, teachers and lessons with my prayers. I discover more clearly God's total control and grip on all situations as I literally surround events and places with my feet as well as my prayers!

We can more realistically appreciate the extent of what we pray for when we specifically surround an area in prayer. Jesus prayed for the city of Jerusalem as he stood overlooking it. We are not often able to overlook towns, but we can surround London in prayer as we drive around the M25. We can consult our Ordnance Survey map for the boundaries of our home towns and take a day or so to walk or run around them, praying specifically and making ourselves familiar with the needs and character of the area. As we walk, run, cycle or drive, God is right there beside us opening our eyes to his wider perspective of our country and land.

One bright spring morning I had been walking for three hours discovering how varied the land was that our town of Christchurch covered. I had set off early through sleeping streets and skirting the River Stour had passed shops just opening. As I crossed Christchurch quay, the Priory in all its magnificence appeared against the sky and the castle ruins made pleasant surroundings for my prayer walk. Over two bridges, past the town hall and sports centre. Our councillors and leisure activities all need to be prayed for and the variety of buildings prompted subjects and needs for prayer. Purewell, Stanpit, Mudeford. What had before been merely areas on a map now became filled with people all needing specific prayer.

In our fast-moving, car-orientated generation, we distance ourselves from people. A wave from our safe little box on wheels saves us from close conversation and a toot on our horn replaces time in companionship. Jesus came to this earth to rub shoulders with and invest time in his people. He knew their needs and spent time with them. If we are to pray intelligently and specifically, we must get among the people who live around us.

Mudeford Quay, usually teaming with tourists, was strangely desolate on this early spring morning and I realised the next stretch of boundary was along the beach to Avon, Friars Cliff and Highcliffe Castle. I continued in prayer for Christchurch when God dramatically widened my vision. With the sea to my right and the land to my left, I suddenly realised this was not just a boundary of Christchurch but also of England and further still the British Isles. How God longs to teach us to pray for our town and our land! Let's get out there and allow him to do it! A neighbourhood watch area can be far more effective if you add the dimension of prayer, producing a watch and pray area. Your church's visitation programme could take off when surrounded by those 'pounding the beat' in prayer. Pornographic shops and other centres that threaten the area's moral health can be closed by surrounding the area with spiritual warfare.

Instead of allowing our inward perspective to paralyse our prayers, let's give God the opportunity to renew and transform our minds. Then interfering with becomes interceding, panic will be replaced by peace and fretting will have no place as God's quiet confidence spurs us on to be watchers and prayers for him. 'I have posted watchmen on your walls, O Jerusalem. They will never be silent day or night. You who call on the Lord give yourselves no rest and give him no rest until he establishes Jerusalem and makes her the praise of the earth' (Is 62:6).

Workout session

Alone

(1) If you have problems with concentration when praying, try a 'distraction list'. Note down any wandering thoughts and get back to prayer. Keep the list for later action.

(2) Explore immediate specific prayer when watching or reading the news. Cut out photographs or headlines from the paper to pin up on a strategically placed peg board as a constant reminder to pray through the day. Eg, 'IRAQ INVADES KUWAIT!'

(3) 'We take captive every thought to make it obedient to Christ' (2 Cor 10:5b). Start a regular exercise of capturing any destructive thoughts such as criticism, immorality and envy.

Confessing them verbally to God, or writing them down for him, helps us to be specific. Then ask God to start his transformation process on your heart and mind so that particular thoughts become obedient to him. From destructive thoughts emerge constructive prayers.

(4) Send a card or letter of encouragement rather than criticise.

In groups

(1) Set up a neighbourhood 'watch and pray' area. In twos or threes walk around and through the streets, houses and shops, praying for individual people, families

and situations. Remember 'watch' does not stand for nosiness or gossip. There should be respect for privacy and confidentiality in your groups.

(2) After a week of watching or reading the news, pool your prayer items. Collectively bring to God the headlines of the week. Keep your prayers brief and to the point, like the headlines.

(3) Surround your children's school in a prayer walk as you return home one morning. Pray for the children, teachers and the board of governors.

(4) Get involved at your local sports centre or evening classes. As you enjoy the activity with friends, pray for the staff and areas in which you can get involved.

(5) If applicable, get involved with your PTA so you can pray knowledgeably to the heart of situations in your local schools.

Recommended reading

Alex Buchanan, *Bible Meditation* (Kingsway: Eastbourne)
Graham Kendrick & John Houghton, *Prayerwalking* (Kingsway: Eastbourne, 1990)

7

Filthy but Forgiven

A further cause of spiritual deafness is the presence of sin. The storm was raging. The winds had reached hurricane force as our channel ferry took the full blast of a freak gale on its return to Dover. The last boat to be allowed across before the height of the storm, our vessel was at the mercy of the elements. After a tiring day driving through France, our family had settled down for the night suddenly to experience a violent storm. I could not believe that such a large boat could be thrown about in all directions without turning over. I was told that the crew were very skilled and in control. This could not be said of my stomach! I was fast losing control of the heaving motion that my insides were being subjected to. Closing my eyes and with an arm around each of my young sons, I was determined to discipline the churning action within and encourage the lads to sleep. Only a very few minutes passed before a voice from beneath my right arm whispered, 'I think I must be sea-sick.' The little green face that peered up at me proved to be my undoing. We all fled for the deck!

Previous experience of this unpleasant condition showed that to be out in the fresh air adjusting to the surrounding landmarks and moving with the action of the vessel quickly restored my equilibrium. Hope faded as the night wind battered my cheeks.

All was pitch black! No lights, no moon and no comforting horizon to stabilise and calm my whirling head and aching stomach. We crouched in a miserable huddle, waiting longingly to reach the firm security of the English coast. Never have lights been more welcome or shelter so peaceful as those of Dover Harbour on that August night. The shrieking wind subsided, and the inky nothingness was filled with concrete shapes and solid, balanced life.

Hours later, in the warm soapiness of a bath, I washed away the filth of that nightmare crossing. To empty a French breakfast, lunch and tea over the side of a rolling ship into the face of hurricane force winds is a pastime I never wish to repeat. The bliss of that bath will not be forgotten. Not until I had sunk right beneath that water, head and all, for the final rinse of my hair did I feel fresh and clean and able to sleep after twenty-four hours of exhausting travel.

Living is often exhausting and messy in the unpredictable journey of life. The calms can seem very few and far between the pitching storms and driving aggravations. To be thrown about from pillar to post at the mercy of circumstance and luck seems an empty existence and a futile philosophy. The Bible states clearly that this is not God's intention. His initial creation was a man and woman, persons of perfect balance physically, mentally and spiritually because of the complete and fulfilling relationship they had with their Creator.

However, the human race chose to go it alone. The breaking of that relationship with God resulting in sin-sickness—a debilitating imbalance that deprives us of spiritual life and leaves us forging through the breakers of life with all that human skill can discover, invent and achieve, but without the divine director to channel that unleashed power.

Without the light of God's presence, our world is thrown into the confusion of wars, child abuse, AIDS, hatred and pain. This kingdom of darkness obliterates any horizon of hope and stability to calm down our topsy-turvy world. The worst memory of our channel crossing was the darkness. I lost all sense of direction and security. It reminds me of 'the raging ocean that covered everything engulfed in total darkness' (Gen 1:2, GNB) before God created light. Then step by step, order came out of chaos through his command and design. Day and night, morning and evening, sky and earth, sea and sand, moon and stars. These have never failed to function. The sun rises and the morning arrives as surely as the earth continues to spin securely around the sun. Only man disrupted the perfect plan, resulting in the chaotic irresponsibility experienced today.

The colossal powercut of all time was when man turned his back on God, his Creator, and cut off all communication with him. In that moment he shut off spiritual light, warmth, communication and sustenance from a never-failing supply of energy. However, God has not left us to stumble around in darkness, hopelessly blind to the meaning of our years spent on this earth. God speaks personally to us through his written word, the Bible, which has been miraculously protected down through the centuries. He broke through time and space to visit us personally as man. John 1:4 speaks of Jesus being 'the word made flesh and dwelling among us'. He was the source of life and this life brought light to mankind. Jesus himself says, 'I am the light of the world.'

As Jesus enters our lives, his light restores balance and reason to life. That living light was extinguished brutally on the cross, choked out by our sin which he took upon himself voluntarily in order to deal once and for all with our sick society. 'It was about twelve o'clock when the sun stopped shining and darkness covered the whole country until three o'clock. Jesus cried out in a loud voice, "Father in your hands I place my Spirit." He said this and died' (Lk 23:44, 46). Our individual acceptance of God ruling our lives in our day to day activities and the Spirit guiding each step of the way allows the light that was temporarily extinguished at Calvary to shine again through us into streets, offices, schools and homes. Wherever we are, God can direct his life and light through us to a dark and disorientated world.

A recent visit to the West Country after a heavy snow fall, left my car encrusted with salt and a film of clinging mud. The windscreen wipers struggled to cope with the spray of filth thrown up from the road, and I was more than relieved to reach my destination. The return journey proved more tricky. Darkness was falling as our stream of traffic hit the motorway. Struggling to peer through the gathering gloom, I turned up the headlights to no avail. The usual shaft of necessary light was not operating. The full beam, normally a dangerous dazzle for oncoming traffic, appeared pathetic and ineffectual. What a night for an electrical fault! Driving was fast becoming impossible, and I crawled into the next service area and sat miserable and cold. Flicking the switches on, I got out into the freezing night air to inspect the offending lights. Instead of a powerful penetrating beam, there was a faint glow. This was totally inadequate to guide me home or to announce my presence to other vehicles on the road. I was in fact a hazard to myself and everyone else on that wintery night. As I tried to sort out my predicament, I absent-mindedly cleaned the windscreen and wing mirrors. Circling round to the front of the car, I flicked the cloth across the lights. A beam of light shot through! Because of the adverse weather conditions the grime had accumulated thick and fast. It had plastered an even blanket of salt and dirt over the headlamps which had steadily thickened to obliterate the normally piercing light within.

We cannot underestimate the filth that the route through this world throws up at us. God deals with the sin that kept us from a healed relationship with himself at conversion, there is no doubt about that. We have eternal life because of what Jesus did, and no one can take that from us. However, for us to hear God's voice, to recognise, obey and allow his light to shine uninterruptedly and clearly through us, we need a continual clean-up routine. The headlamps through which his life and light can announce his presence to the world are our individual lives and the united life of the church. The initial clean-up and turn-around at conversion that we read of in 1 Corinthians 1:2—'To the church of God in Corinth, to those sanctified in Christ Jesus and called to be holy' must be accompanied by the ongoing cleansing work of the Holy Spirit—'May the God who gives us peace, make you holy in every way, and keep your whole being spirit, soul and body ... free from every fault at the coming of our Lord Jesus Christ' (1 Thess 5:23).

Anything that comes between God and us is going to stifle his voice. It is the cleaning up of those wrong attitudes, habits, relationships and situations that we so often try to solve ourselves, or give up on. Neglect of the tiniest fault can have disastrous and far-reaching effects.

It is often the apparently hidden mistakes that eventually have the worst consequences.

Beneath the floorboards of a newly built house, a small nail had been hammered a fraction short of its intended destination. Instead of securing a floorboard it came to rest in a water pipe beneath. Before the central heating system came into operation in the first autumn, the error went undetected. The nail in fact prevented any leakage while it rested securely in the hole it had mistakenly made. The disaster came when the heat was on. Under the pressure the pipe expanded and the nail popped out of the enlarged hole. Silently the steady flow of water filled the under-floor cavity and seeped through the ceiling of the room beneath. Because the new tenant had not moved in, the seeping moisture was not discovered until days later when we waded through the living room to discover the devastation. We summoned a plumber to search for and mend the offending pipe and started the long task of mopping up the murky water.

It was in the darkness of the cupboard under the stairs, ankle deep in water and with freezing hands that I realised just how much time and heartache could have been saved if that tiny error with all its potential destruction could have been discovered and dealt with in the earlier days. An army of workmen have put to right the damage that tiny nail made, but that house stands as a constant reminder of the vital, searching work God wants to do in me. When I invited him into my life, it wasn't for a cosy, complacent salvation which shouts to the world, 'I'm all right Jack!' The ongoing work of cleansing must allow him into every room of my daily living. His all-seeing eyes see right beneath the floorboards and into the locked cupboards. He is aware of the inevitable damage that lies ahead if a wrong relationship continues or bad habits aren't broken. Attitudes need to be changed and laziness swept away.

The prayer in Psalm 139:23–24 is a tough one and should not be uttered lightly. A translation from the Chinese has particularly brought home the power of this prayer: 'O God, examine me (as in the Customs), test my inmost thoughts, intentions and meanings. Look right inside me (X-ray me) and see if there is hate, evil in my being. You may take my hand along the heavenly way.'

Shortly after the Lockerbie air disaster of 1989, I was travelling to Detroit, Michigan. As I approached the Customs area, a security guard drew alongside me and my luggage and started a search that left me very thankful I had nothing to hide. Every article of clothing was unfolded and shaken out. Each container from soap to jewel box was opened and checked for hidden compartments. My toilet bag was emptied and each intimate item studied. I felt stripped and vulnerable. If it hadn't been for the friendly reminder from the security guard that this was for my protection and benefit, a guard against the devastating and lethal results of hidden bombs, I could have been put off travelling for life.

Sin has a disastrous effect on our lives. Whether commencing unseen and apparently with no harm in our thoughts, the progressive effect is lethal. 'Each one is tempted when by his own evil desire, he is dragged away and enticed. Then, after desire has conceived, it gives birth to sin, and sin when it is full grown, gives birth to death' (Jas 1:14–15). There is no doubt about the attraction of sin—Satan has to make it so enticing because it all ends in death. 'O God, examine me (as in the Customs).' If we make a practice of using this prayer in our growing relationship with God and obey his loving correction and direction, there may well be some painful adjustments to make, but in the long run God will save us all the agony of the accumulated disaster of unconfessed sin which can eventually blow us apart and affect so many lives, spilling over to touch even our next generation.

Before destructive introspection destroys any hope of enjoying our Christian life, remember it is the work of the Holy Spirit to cleanse us continually. God never brings to our attention any disorder in our lives that he is not able to supply the power for us to overcome or remove it.

On the fourth day of a family holiday in Portugal, I was just beginning to unwind. I had slept, swum, sunbathed and done precious little else. When you are in a close relationship to someone, loving silence is a necessary ingredient for companionship. However, when it is neglect and forgetfulness it is not long before we try to capture their attention. It was through my eldest son that God in fact demanded my attention. Stephen was lying prostrate on his bed reading, his sunburnt back freshly creamed. 'James talks a lot of sense,' he grunted. Silence . . . 'James who?' I absent-mindedly questioned. 'This one,' he said, holding up his Bible at the New Testament book of James. 'Oh!' was my eloquent reply.

The sight of that book was God's finger probing into the careless area of my heart, for I had completely switched off from his presence in the excitement of the holiday that he had in fact provided. As the family spilled out of the apartment for a swim, I retrieved my Bible from the suitcase and opened it at James. I was eventually to devour the whole of that book as I realised how spiritually hungry I was after my neglect of God.

Much of my time, however, was spent in James 1:21— 'So get rid of every filthy habit and all wicked conduct. Submit to God and accept the word that he plants in your heart which is able to save you.' In this society, filthy habits and wicked conduct immediately suggest obvious and gross sins like child and drug abuse, rape and murder. I didn't need these brought to my attention. We were enjoying a break from the constant reminder of the media.

What God did remind me of was Isaiah 64:6 (AV)—
'All our righteousnesses are as filthy rags.' The Good
News Bible reads: 'All of us have been sinful; even our
best actions are filthy through and through.' If it was our
sin that nailed Jesus to the cross and caused him so much
agony of mind and spirit, can you imagine what he goes
through dwelling in a life that is still harbouring these
filthy rags? What about the critical spirit, the thoughtless
gossip, pride and the second-hand violence and immorality we allow into our living rooms through the television?

Thankfully James doesn't stop at the filthy habits and
wicked conduct, he goes on to give God's perfect solution
for living the victorious Christian life: 'Submit to God
and accept the word that he plants in your hearts, which
is able to save you' (Jas 1:21, GNB). This takes our eyes
away from ourselves, and away from earthly techniques
and formulas to eradicate sin. It fixes our eyes fairly and
squarely on God and all his ability to release us from the
bondage of sin.

As I sat thinking these things over, with my Bible open
at last, I discovered again the power of the written word of
God. I asked him again to increase my hunger for it. I had
neglected memorising it for some time and realised afresh,
as I embedded the words in my memory, that this exercise
helps in the step of obedience actually to 'accept the word
which God plants in our hearts which is able to save you'.

I found myself humming a tune learnt from Ishmael's
'Glories' at Spring Harvest: 'I have hidden your word in
my heart that I might not sin against you. I have hidden
your word in my heart that I might not sin against you.
That I might not sin against you, that I might not sin
against you. I have hidden your word in my heart that I
might not sin against you.' These words from Psalm
119:11 have been set to a catchy tune which youngsters
can pick up easily. They came readily to my memory and
their impact shook me.

We underestimate the power and protection within the pages of the Bible. If we realised its full potential we would have stored it away in our memories long ago, and would not wait until it is taken from us as in countries where the Bible is confiscated. We would be working it out continually in our daily life, obeying the command in James 1:22—'Do not deceive yourselves by just listening to his word; instead put it into practice!' (GNB).

Workout session

Alone

(1) In our natural conversation with God we can sometimes lose sight of his holiness, majesty and greatness. Before each time with God, develop a period of preparation. Make sure there is nothing hindering your relationship. Using the prayer in Psalm 139:23–24, list any inmost thoughts, intentions and meanings which are selfish and not of God. Let God's X-ray eye root out any specific hate and evil, and ask him to cleanse you and refresh you. Then, literally without anything in between, let God take your hand for a time together unspoilt by unconfessed sin.

Note: a time of preparation often leads to action—a phone call to apologise; a letter received that has been forgotten. Practise immediate obedience and action where possible. 'Procrastination is the thief of time.' It is also a tool of Satan!

(2) Turn-out day in the garage or junk room. As you

turn out accumulated rubbish from home or office, parallel it with a spiritual clean-out session. Finish with a bonfire or a visit to a council tip.

Group activity

(1) Have a time of praise and worship together using, where possible, hymns and choruses that are literally the word of God set to music. Eg, *Scripture in Song*.

(2) Discuss how our lives can accumulate dirt from our day-to-day experiences. Eg, some papers and magazines, some programmes and adverts on the television.

(3) Share practical ways of avoiding this build-up of filth, such as learning to be selective in viewing television.

(4) Collectively or in pairs, pray for each other's protection in specific areas.

Recommended reading

Derek Page, *You Can Overcome Temptation* (SU/Saltmine)
Charles Price, *Christ for Real* (Marshall and Pickering)

8

Hugging Our Hurts

The presence of sin definitely handicaps our communication with God. However, pain and suffering can have the opposite effect. If given to God, he can speak clearly through it rather than allowing it to cripple us.

My heartbeat seemed to echo down the darkened corridors of the hospital as Doug and I raced to the outpatients' department where our eldest son lay unconscious, wrapped in tin-foil like a turkey trussed ready for the oven. I screamed inwardly at the incongruous sight, instinct causing me to assure him everything would be all right now I was there. The air was empty, the accusing eyes of the nurses and doctors were my only answer as they tended to their senseless patient.

A choking love welled up inside me as I stared down at his motionless form. His eyes were closed, his breathing heavy. Memories flooded back of the numerous times when he was younger that I had tucked him into bed and kissed him. Tonight was a cruel contrast. This was no peaceful sleep—he was out, stone-cold drunk! The unwelcome words shattered my usual complacency as I sat stiffly in the impersonal waiting-room. Now was not the time to be told, almost triumphantly, that Stephen could have died inhaling his own vomit. I felt sick.

One o'clock in the morning was a lonely hour for heart-searching, and the accusing questions came thick and fast. Where had we gone wrong? What would people think? Was this just a horrific nightmare from which I would awake? Later as we mounted the stairs to the Observation Ward where he was to stay the night, I struggled with facing the facts. My golden-haired first-born was a natural teenager who made mistakes. I wrestled with my own inadequacy in knowing how best to help him as Doug coaxed me away from his bedside so that an emerging man could wake up alone to his mistake and accompanying hangover.

That night was the longest, loneliest night of my life. I sat bolt upright in bed and faced my failure, feeling useless and out of control. Unlike a number of my friends, I had enjoyed parenthood, from birth through the early years, and prided myself on two strapping youngsters. My fast-fading positive approach to the teen years finally disappeared with this episode. To be told that Stephen had been the victim of a teenager's joke did not dilute my dejection. Outwardly I coped with mechanical maturity, inwardly I was empty, lost and strangely alone in my failure. My usual ability to organise and talk people round was malfunctioning. With every corner I turned in my daily life I was confronted by another memory of failure and guilt. Any achievements paled into insignificance. I was fit for nothing!

That phrase had dogged my footsteps throughout life. Usually a playful remark relating to my enjoyment of sport, its negativism now crippled my normal positive approach to life. My thoughts raced back through the years to a lonely figure in a deserted school cloakroom. My easy coping with life had just been shattered by those well-worn words 'You are fit for nothing!' My coat-crowded refuge hid my despair. In those impressionable years, I had bounced back with a fighting spirit to prove all the teachers wrong. My love of sport and team competition had motivated me to fulfil my potential in the teaching profession. 'Fit for nothing' went far deeper these many years later. They cut right through selfish ambition and personal dreams to the very heart of my personality. They swept aside what I could do to reveal the real me—a nobody!

An unusual weariness crept through me as the familiar verses of Scripture seemed to mock my mental struggle: 'We know that in all things God works for good with those who love God' (Rom 8:28, GNB). Perhaps I didn't love him enough? 'Let not your heart be troubled, you believe in God—believe also in me.' Perhaps I didn't believe enough? A destructive self-examination ensued that, long after the incident that had caused it had passed, caused me to question my capabilities and specifically my deteriorating communication with our two teenage sons.

Throughout my life I had been thrown into many different situations and had learned early to adjust. In fact I almost welcomed challenge and crisis in order to stretch my ability and ingenuity to adapt. This was different. I was hurting and bewildered, the challenge was no longer enjoyable, the crisis too close to home. My discovery that prayer was a two-way conversation with God, my living Creator, not just cold formality, was being stretched to its limit. The continual complaints and cries for help received no immediate answer as I wore myself out trying to solve the hassles and meet the demands.

The day was stormy, the house deserted, as I approached our well-worn settee with my steaming mug of coffee. I identified fondly with my favourite piece of furniture—much used, frayed at the edges, and sagging under the weight of a very active family and friends. As I sipped silently the tears started rolling. I had hit rock bottom. I wept out my frustration, inadequacy and weakness to a God who had waited so patiently for me to give up my independent fight. I leafed through the pages of my Bible desperately. 'While she was sitting there she began to cry.' I had been reading in Genesis 21 the day before and these words in verse 16 captured my attention. I immediately identified with Hagar in her tears and even more so when I discovered she was weeping because of her son and her inadequacy to help him. I read hurriedly on to find God speaking directly to me alongside Hagar. 'What are you troubled about Hagar? Don't be afraid. God has heard the boy crying. Get up, go and pick him up and comfort him.'

The excitement of hearing God speak directly to me was mixed with an impatience in recognising that he had hit the nail on the head. My inadequacy stemmed from the fact that I could no longer pick up and comfort grown teenagers. If only they were babies again! There had been no problems in those days in comforting and controlling. As the storm outside cleared towards evening and the sun shone through, so God had calmed my fiery spirit and his patient wisdom had broken through my proud resolve.

A whole new education lay before me. It was not for me to teach my teenagers but for God to open up my eyes to his resources to solve the problems. I had to take opportunities to encourage, guide and comfort Stephen and Duncan as men, not children. Picking up and comforting became days of fishing on the end of a pier, last-minute dashes to the airport for the registration numbers of aircraft, asking and acting on their advice, allowing them the freedom of making mistakes and being around to support them on the rebound. The secret lies in verses 19 and 20 of Genesis 21. Because of my argumentative spirit, I missed the vital provision for our fit-for-nothing situations on that stormy day, and God allowed me to experience it before I read it. 'Then God opened her eyes and she saw a well. She went and filled the leather bag and gave some to the boy. God was with the boy as he grew up.'

I needed my eyes opened to the resources that God was longing to give. When our eyes are riveted on our inadequacy and weakness, we are choked spiritually and crippled by other people's opinions and condemnation. What other people think becomes more important than what God says. James 1:5 (GNB) states loud and clear: 'If any of you lacks wisdom he should pray to God, who will give it to him.' Our acknowledged limitation allows God's wisdom to operate in our lives—and he doesn't just give wisdom, he 'gives generously and graciously to all'!

There is a growing urgency for Christians to reach out to a suspicious world. Because of the days in which we live, a complete generation is growing up strongly encouraged to trust and accept no one. Mankind's struggle is to live in a far from ideal world. Violence, sickness, AIDS, child abuse, famine, disaster and the fact of death continually erode our self-confidence and ability to cope with, let alone enjoy, our humanity. Many in their fight for survival turn to drink, drugs and the occult. An increasing number lose the fight in suicide. So where is the God who says, 'I have come that they may have life and have it to the full' (Jn 10:10)? Sadly, as millions clutch at straws for survival, he is hidden in the lives of Christians crushed by inadequacy, cramped by weakness and crippled by pain and hurt.

A favourite cake in our family is the crusty lemon bake: a light lemon sponge coated in lemon juice and crisp with sugar. Each time I make it I am fascinated by the limp remains of the lemon skin. Before baking, the fruit is full, round and firm. After the cutting, squeezing and grating it is limp, empty and torn, only fit for the dustbin. Do you feel like that at times? Torn apart, drained and literally wrung out by the challenges, pressures and problems of life: family, job, unemployment, sickness, bereavement, promotion, church responsibilities, loneliness. With each twist and turn of our daily lives our nerves are grated to shreds and our spirits are crushed.

God has experienced through his thirty-three years on this earth the most exhausting times physically, spiritually, mentally and socially. He endured rejection, criticism, misunderstanding, disappointment and wrongful accusation.

It was with a mixture of powerful emotions that I watched the torture and eventual mob-killing of two young soldiers in Northern Ireland on our television screens. My feelings ranging from panic to outrage, I struggled with the clinging images of that incident for many days. The memory of a mob-killing in AD 33 has provoked a wide-ranging mixture of emotions down through 2,000 years, from cold indifference to burning passion. The fact remains—Jesus gave himself willingly to a mob-killing that he could have stopped at any time. How I longed on that fateful day in Ireland, that with the flick of my television switch I could have stopped that butchery.

As God walked this earth as the man Jesus, at any time during his thirty-three years he could have thrown the switch on his whole plan of salvation. Those thirty-three years were just as much a sacrifice in life as in his death. The evening before his crucifixion, we have a powerful reminder of his human frailty as he pleads in prayer in the Garden of Gethsemane, '"Father, if you will take this cup of suffering from me, not my will however, but your will be done." ... In great anguish he prayed even more fervently; his sweat was like great drops of blood falling to the ground.' Jesus had an appointment with death itself. He set it and he kept it.

Then from the cold confines of the tomb and hell itself, Jesus burst out in resurrection power, proving his words to us in John 10:10—'I have come that they may have life and have it to the full.' The cross is empty! The tomb is empty! God's risen strength can fill our weakness. His fullness of life can occupy our hollow emptiness.

When everyone seems to misunderstand us and we are so weary of trying to justify ourselves, Jesus' risen strength is made perfect in our weakness. When the demands on our time are mounting and we grow so tired of people, his risen strength is made perfect in our weakness. When bereavement drains the very motivation for living out of us, his risen strength is made perfect in our weakness. When failure dogs our footsteps and mistakes glare us in the face, his risen strength is made perfect in our weakness. When pain racks our body and we long to be out of it, his risen strength is made perfect in our weakness. When all our plans and dreams are dashed to the ground, his risen strength is made perfect in our weakness. When we feel isolated and alone and no one seems to understand, his risen strength is made perfect in our weakness.

In 2 Corinthians 12:7, Paul describes his weakness very pointedly as his thorn in his flesh. He pleads three times with the Lord to remove it from him, but the Lord says very clearly to him, 'My grace is sufficient for you, for my power is made perfect in weakness' (2 Cor 12:9). Later in Ephesians 1:19, we read that that 'power is like the working of his mighty strength, which he exerted in Christ when he raised him from the dead'.

As individuals and as a family we are learning to hug our hurts. That is not to say we deliberately ask for them or glory in them, but in our acceptance of each other and our weaknesses and the various continuing crises, lies a God-given peace as he pours his power into our weakness. This power does not need to impress others, but allows us to rest securely in God buying back every failure and hurt, as well as each success and achievement, for his plan. It is one of the devil's most devious lies that we are fit for nothing. It is our confessed inadequacy that is the most effective qualification to serve a God who died to have his risen strength made perfect in our weakness. No past experience, memory or confessed sin should prevent us from the exciting potential that God has planned for us.

Although God's redemptive work of salvation was finalised on the cross, his only means of living communication with the world is through us. This involves a continual release of his life through ours in an ongoing relationship through prayer. It is vital that the devil does not get hold of our failures and weaknesses. Our pain and bereavement, misunderstanding and jealousies are mangled and magnified beyond all recognition when he gets his dirty hands on them. If God can take our sin, with all its filth, to show his love, can he not also with that same resurrection power take our painful experiences and hurting years and turn them inside out to produce an army of ordinary people with an extraordinary God who speaks to and through us to reach a fit-for-nothing world?

Workout session

Alone

(1) Write down a fit-for-nothing experience of the past or present. This can be a painful exercise and if tears come during it, give them to God as a literal outpouring of wordless prayer. Tears are more expressive than words to a God who collects them as powerful expressions of our inmost being.

(2) Memorise 2 Corinthians 12:9—'My grace is sufficient for you, for my power is made perfect in weakness.' Remind yourself of this verse every time you feel weak. Practise making God's power perfect in prayer. Give your weakness to God instead of letting it cripple you, and ask him to fill it with his power. For example, pray 'Father I give you my jealousy of John and his ability.' Or, 'Lord, take my heartache over my children.' Writing down our prayers can help us to identify a weakness that we are very good at disguising.

The breathing exercises of Chapter 5 will help practically in crises. Breathing in God's strength and expelling our weakness is an outward expression of the inward spiritual exercise.

(3) List the main causes that stop you praying, such as tiredness or pain.

Group activity

(1) Share your 'fit-for-nothing' experience, either by speaking about it spontaneously, or reading what you have written. This is not compulsory as deep hurts are difficult to share. As you grow in confidence with one other person, this can be a release leading to prayer.

(2) Discuss practical ways of 'picking up and comforting' each other. Eg, be a listening ear.

Recommended reading

Philip Yancey, *Where Is God When It Hurts?* (Pickering and Inglis)
Warren Wiersbe, *Why Us?* (IVP)
Mark Simmons, *You Can Share Your Faith* (SU/Saltmine)

9

Heart to Heart

I sat shivering, a ridiculous figure on a normally sun-drenched villa roof! Having waved off my friends at 6.00am from my vantage point, I decided to wait for the sun to rise. I couldn't remember the last time I had seen dawn break, but I was fast becoming impatient for the warmth and light that rapidly became excessive when on holiday in Portugal. My eyes were drawn, as if by a magnet, to the hill behind the villa. The trees were etched darkly against the rose-tinted sky which was becoming brighter by the minute. To hasten the arrival, I clambered up the sloping roof and stood on tiptoe, my eyes raking the hilltop for the first glimmer of the sun's entrance. The trees stood silent, seemingly mocking my reckless impatience, and I slithered down from my precarious perch. My longing increased as I waited, realising I had lived for approximately 17,000 days but couldn't remember having waited to see the sun rise.

Gone are the days when we have to get up and go to bed with the sun. Central heating, electric lighting, crop-growing aids and cooking facilities have all assisted in our comfort, but have also caused us to forget how vital and necessary the sun is to our life and growth. We cannot live without the sun, yet we comment on it flippantly when it is hidden behind clouds or when it penetrates the ozone layer. As I waited overlooking a shadowed countryside, I became acutely aware that in our progressive society this independent attitude seeps into all areas. We cannot live without the risen Son of God. He gives us physical and spiritual life. Every single breath we take is because God allows it, and yet so often we only vehemently acknowledge him when he seems absent, when disaster falls or when he penetrates our carefully guarded personal lives with his challenge to perfection.

Prayer is starting the day and finishing it with the risen Son of God. It is the very practical recognition of his continual presence with us and our utter dependence on him. It is an ongoing relationship which involves us waiting in his presence and listening to what he is going to say to us and with us. As that first sliver of gold crept over the hill and cast its golden beams across the countryside, bringing light and warmth, so God's presence and voice comes to every listening ear, transforming lives and shedding light on the way ahead. We do not have a silent God. He speaks through his written word, his creation, his men and women. Through the prophetic word, the word of knowledge, and by means of dreams, pictures and visions. He uses our thoughts, imagination and daily experiences to draw our attention to his longing to communicate with us. He is not necessarily going to use all these avenues to speak to us, but the one unique channel for all of us is God's word, the Bible. It is essential to dig deep into this living Book, to hear God speak and to know that all the other channels through which a creative mighty God still speaks, will be in line and supported by Scripture.

From the first chapter of Genesis to the last chapter of Revelation, our God is a God who speaks. He communicates clearly in many varied and colourful ways, and Scripture is saturated with his living voice in a two-way relationship with those he has created. From intimate talks with Adam and Eve while walking in the Garden of Eden, we see him communicating directly and continually with Noah to open up a way of escape from the flood. Abraham, described as the 'friend of God', was familiar with God's voice. Among the many words of God recorded to him is the promise that he will be the father of the great nation of Israel against all odds. God talked at great length and in intricate detail to this ninety-nine-year-old man to reveal his plans which included him (Genesis 17 and 18).

Israel was the grandson of Abraham. If Abraham had been alive in the days when Israel was called Jacob, I'm sure he would have despaired of his offspring's scheming and deceit, and wondered if God had made a mistake. But God can see beyond family frustrations; he has a panoramic view of a perfect plan that interweaves all our faults and failings as well as our mighty moments. God spoke unexpectedly to Jacob in a dream, causing him to wake and say, 'Surely the Lord is in this place and I was not aware of it' (Gen 28:16). Jacob was again to meet with God many years later after the birth of his son Joseph to Rachel, his second wife. This time it was no dream, but a face-to-face confrontation as he wrestled for God's blessing. After having his name changed to Israel, he called the scene of the struggle Peniel saying, 'It is because I saw God face to face and yet my life was spared' (Gen 32:30).

His son Joseph had a disrupted life of family love and

hatred. He was kidnapped, sold into slavery, wrongly accused and imprisoned. This catalogue of catastrophe is punctuated with the constant reminder that 'the Lord was with Joseph'. God not only communicated with Joseph in the well-known dreams of his youth, but in the pit of despair, in a foreign land, and when seemingly forgotten in prison. His endurance and consistency, which eventually saw him as Prime Minister in Egypt directing famine relief, was the result of his two-way relationship with a God who speaks to and sustains us in the most dark and prolonged episodes in our lives.

So Joseph's family are united in Egypt before his father, now called Israel, died. God continued to fulfil his personal promise to Abraham, Isaac and Jacob to make them a great nation, and their numbers rapidly multiplied 'so that the land was filled with them' (Ex 1:6b).

With the death of Joseph and his whole generation came a new Pharaoh who knew nothing of Joseph. The fear in his heart was the land riddled with foreigners, a threat to his nation. So started the tough slavery of the children of Israel in a land that was not theirs. God's systematic and powerful plan ran through, involving men and women listening and talking to him. Moses led the increasing nation of Israel out of Egypt, surviving all the obstacles Pharaoh threw at him because of his confrontation with God and hearing his voice calling to him personally out of a burning bush in the desert at Horeb (Ex 3:4; 4:17). His continual lengthy dialogue with God brought him through the traumas of forty years in the wilderness to die just before his assistant and successor Joshua led Israel into their promised land of Canaan.

God's personal and direct words commence the Book of Joshua and right through his life we see God in constant consultation with his man for the moment. They talked together through military strategy and the governing of the tribes of Israel. Joshua completed

Moses' work in close communication with God, establishing Israel in the promised land of Canaan.

There followed a period of 325 years when heroic men and women called judges ruled Israel, including a courageous lady called Deborah. She had a remarkable relationship with God who gave her insight and confidence through her continual consultation with him. The history of Israel unfolds through the following books of the Old Testament. Right throughout the ups and downs of their history, when Israel listened God's voice could be heard through judges, kings and prophets. The child Samuel cried, 'Speak Lord for your servant hears;' he was the means by which Solomon and David became the first kings of Israel. In Job 40–24 we see Job and the Lord in desperate dialogue; this is a powerful illustration of the advisability of listening to God before others. After all Job's suffering, he said to God, 'You said, "Listen now, and I will speak; I will question you and you shall answer me." My ears had heard of you, but now my eyes have seen you' (Job 42:4–5). The Psalms are a perfect example of God's two-way conversation with the Psalmist.

The prophets heard and spoke God's voice, both in judgement and restoration, in anger and in mercy, and we always see the ache in God's heart to reveal his love. Time and time again we see the victorious results of listening to and obeying God's voice.

God's most eloquent and powerful communication with us was when he came himself in the person of his Son, the Lord Jesus Christ. His living word was clothed in flesh and came and lived with us, was killed by us and rose again for us—a cry wrung from God's heart and written in the life, death and resurrection of Jesus; a cry which says, 'I love you this much!' Our God spoke yesterday, he speaks today, and he continues to speak— 'Jesus Christ, the same yesterday, today and for ever'

(Heb 13:8). He does not need to add to Scripture for the Bible is complete in doctrine, but he speaks through it freshly and specifically for our everyday lives in the twentieth century. 'All scripture is God breathed and is useful for teaching, rebuking, correcting and training in righteousness, so that the man of God may be thoroughly equipped for every good work' (2 Tim 3:16–17). We need to dig deep into the word of God and mine the wisdom and truth within its pages, hiding it within our hearts to draw on at every possible opportunity.

Right now I am enjoying a very weird and wonderful relationship which fluctuates between fascination and frustration. My emotions see-saw daily between intriguing wonder and explosive rage. Neighbours hear me bursting from my home letting off steam verbally one minute, and are puzzled the next to hear the anger transformed into terms of endearment. I look constantly for the object of my affection, introducing him to all who visit my home, but my impatience increases as this strange friendship grows.

It is autumn and the leaves are falling. Following the storms tiny acorns have carpeted our pathway. My little grey squirrel is sure he is in heaven. He leaps gleefully from tree to fence, from garage to grass, industriously digging and hiding in my carefully nurtured lawn. He cannot believe the endless store he has and he likes to dig them up, have a nibble, and bury them again elsewhere. His obvious enjoyment and persistent activity have overcome my exasperation. As I have been wrestling with the knowledge that our living God speaks today in a variety of ways, God has taught me through the parable of my squirrel the vital exercise of continually burying his word in our hearts, and allowing him to draw it to our attention. We can dig it out, chew it over and enjoy it afresh, listening to what God says in different situations.

Leafing through my first adventure into writing to God some years back, I came across two verses that had puzzled me in 1 Samuel 3. It was the opening verse and closing verses. Verse 1 states clearly: 'In those days the word of the Lord was rare.' By the time we read down to verse 21 we see that 'the Lord continued to appear at Shiloh, and there he revealed himself to Samuel through his word. And Samuel's words came to all Israel.' The striking contrast between these verses recaptured me as God unearthed scriptures that he needed to apply to my present experience.

What caused God to speak again after his long silence? As I searched through the previous two chapters of 1 Samuel, all I could find was a poor, broken lady. She felt a failure as a wife and mother and over a period of many years was taunted by the other wife, Peninah, for her barrenness. The torment and depression that must have resulted was an agony. But God sees right beneath exteriors to a womb that he had closed (1 Sam 1:5), and to a heart that he had opened. Instead of allowing the bitterness to cripple her, Hannah opened her heart to the Lord continually and poured it all out to him (1 Sam 1:10–12).

Through the years of anguish, Hannah was in a close relationship with her God. He was developing in her a heart that would respond to him, a heart after him. God specialises in the most effective heart surgery, and in order to hear him speak we first of all need to have a *broken heart*. We need to see ourselves and the world as God sees us. We need to appreciate the mangled mess our wayward hearts have got us into and ask God to break our old desires and attitudes and replace them with his wholesome, pure design. A heart that beats steadily and securely, responding to the perfect plan that God has for us even through the most difficult times.

Hannah's long-desired son was born out of the most deep, prolonged suffering. She had learned to be in the continual state of brokenness that we see in Jesus in the

Garden of Gethsemane: 'Father, if you are willing, take this cup from me; yet not my will, but yours be done' (Lk 22:42). Just as the resurrection resulted from Jesus' broken heart, will and body, so out of Hannah's brokenness God not only opened her womb to give her a son, but through that son and her obedience he opens his mouth once more to speak to a nation and to us.

As God looked beyond the external, he saw that Hannah had a *prayerful heart*. Her prayers are *sorrowful*. She didn't allow bitterness and resentment to accumulate and fester, thus hindering her communication with God; she continually poured out her barrenness and brokenness to him. In that vulnerable position before the divine surgeon, she allowed him to purge the poison that destroys and to prepare her for the tough but joyful task ahead. Not only is Hannah's prayer sorrowful, it is also *sacrificial*. This lady meant business, and although her mother's heart ached for her son, she was also willing to commit herself and him to an extremely sacrificial life of total commitment to God. This was no idle, careless promise but a calculated commitment which we see fulfilled in 1 Samuel 1:24–28.

Hannah's prayers are also transparently *specific*. Through the clarity and sharpness of her prayer, we see the work of God in her heart. She expresses God's desire, as well as her own, for a special son who will be committed to God and will speak out once more God's purpose to the nation. The prayers wrung from her heart are sorrowful, sacrificial, specific and lastly, because of her extreme circumstances, they are often *silent*. In 1 Samuel 1:13, we see her brutally misunderstood by Eli the priest. In her agony of prayer, with only her lips moving and her tears flowing, he reproved her for being drunk! 'Not so, my lord,' Hannah replied. 'I am a woman who is deeply troubled. I have not been drinking wine or beer; I was pouring out my soul to the Lord. Do not take your servant for a wicked woman; I have been praying here out of my great anguish and grief' (1 Sam 1:15–16).

God continued his work in Hannah's heart, and through Eli the priest, Hannah heard God speaking peace and hope into her situation (1 Sam 1:17). She trusted God and we see the signs of her tremendously *faithful* heart as, after many years of depression and little appetite, 'she went her way and ate something and her face was no longer downcast' (1 Sam 1:18). Her heart was full of faith, although she had not yet conceived a son.

Samuel's birth and weaning span just a few verses of Scripture, which hide from us the unspeakable joy and fulfilment Hannah must have experienced. What we do read is a whole chapter of explosive rejoicing as Hannah surrenders her one and only young son to live in the Temple with Eli. Her heart was strictly *obedient* to her promise and as a result her heart was filled with joy (1 Sam 2).

As God's eye penetrated the lives of his two servants Hannah and Samuel, he saw hearts that responded to him—broken, prayerful, faithful and obedient hearts. He broke his silence in sovereign power to speak to them as individuals and then through them to the nation.

I have just been chewing over a 'nut', a nugget of truth God gave me a few years back, hidden in my heart. Today he speaks powerfully and relevantly from his living word into my own life, my family life and my church life. 'Speak Lord in the stillness while I wait on thee, hush my heart to listen in expectancy.'

Workout session

These exercises can be done alone or in groups.

(1) Prayer in preparation for approaching God's word and hearing him speak.
   Pray for:
   (a) Cleansing.
   (b) Clarity in thought with no preconceived ideas.
   (c) Control by the Holy Spirit to guide us into all truth.
   (d) Change as I apply Scripture to my life.

(2) Prayer in reading the passage.
   Read silently Ephesians 3:16–21. Underline or note down any verses or ideas that you feel God might be drawing to your attention.

(3) Prayer in proving the passage.
   Share in groups what God has highlighted for you through this passage.
   How does the teaching of this scriptural prayer apply to your day-to-day life?

(4) Prayer in putting it into practice.
   (a) Make this a daily prayer for yourself this week.
   (b) Take a part of this passage and pray it for someone else in your group.

Recommended reading

Floyd McClung, *The Father Heart of God* (Kingsway: Eastbourne)

10
Lost for Words

Tears are a gift. From our first newborn yelps to quiet sobs of bereavement, our physical bodies need the outlet of tears. They are the eloquent language of our deepest feelings. Sadly, in adults they have often been dismissed as weakness, or embarrassingly ignored as lack of control. For someone who did not cry a lot, and certainly not in public, tears were at first an uncomfortable reminder to me that God creates us as whole people and emotions are involved in our relationship with him. Initially, I found it very bewildering and embarrassing to be moved to tears in times of worship and prayer. Hymns I had sung with unconcerned abandon all my life would now break me, and verses of Scripture memorised from childhood now cut deep into my emotions. This appeared to hinder my praying and praise until I discovered this heartsearching prayer of David's: 'You have seen me tossing and turning through the night. You have collected all my tears and preserved them in your bottle! You have recorded every one in your book' (Ps 56:8, TLB). Although David is praying in sorrow in this situation, he reveals clearly that whatever emotion our tears are expressive of, God treasures this eloquent language and understands it.

However diverse our experience, God identifies with it. He is familiar with every flicker of feeling and each pinpoint of pain. He delights in our excitement but also understands guilt and regret. His identification with us is starkly seen in Isaiah 53:3—'He is despised and rejected . . . a man of sorrows and acquainted with grief.' Jesus wept over towns and people. He cried out in acute isolation to a Father who had forsaken him. If Jesus wept, tears should not hinder our communication with God but enhance it. Tears are a gift from God to include in our relationship with the person who created them. It is a biological fact that they are physically beneficial to us. Given immediately to God, they are a sincere sacrifice of our undisguised selves. Yet directed inwardly, they can literally choke and cripple us in self-pity and bitterness.

One such occasion when I was moved to tears was at the International Conference of Itinerant Evangelists in Amsterdam in 1986. Over 100 nations were represented and extensive arrangements had been made for the interpretation of our seminars on the family life of the evangelist. A moving procession of all the nations and their flags brought the congress to a close. As thousands of voices were lifted in that gigantic stadium, a multi-languaged paeon of praise and prayer rose to our God. I alternated between laughter and tears as I started to fathom a great and mighty God above all this apparent confusion of sound. He could hear and understand every single prayer and also interpret every cry from the heart. Our God is not limited by language. His communication is universal and multi-lingual. An extra language suddenly seemed so understandable.

For years I had struggled with a limited knowledge of a scriptural language called 'tongues'. Rumours were rife concerning it when I was at college in the early 1960s. It appeared that a lunatic fringe included it in their vocabulary and experience; ignorance caused me to avoid it. For someone who found severe difficulties with passing my own language at 'O' level, let alone attempting French or German, I knew achieving another language was impossible. I switched off every time the subject came up, or dismissed it as an extreme, rather dubious activity. That was prior to my simple request, 'Lord, teach me to pray.' Slowly God brought his teaching to bear on my life.

I had grown up in an excellent home and church in South London where I was saturated with Scripture from birth. We do not realise how early a child absorbs things from scriptural surroundings. The word of God is not limited to age or ability. Naturally, there were times of boredom through long services, but I soaked up so much teaching that it is only now that I can fully appreciate it. Both my parents were totally involved with their family and church and worked out all knowledge of their God and his word very practically in a home open to all. I grew up surrounded by the coming and going of people from all walks of life. Thoroughly enjoying church life, I was encouraged to get involved, particularly in youth activities.

On arrival at college I desperately missed my home and church. It was at this time of insecurity that I first heard about 'tongues'. Without hesitation I discarded it as unacceptable. I had a very similar experience with sweetcorn several years later! A vital part of my secure home was my mum's cooking. She presented us with meal after meal of varied and beautifully cooked food. Except for sweetcorn. I discovered this nutritious vegetable when I married Doug. To surprise him, I gently boiled

two cobs in salted water, drained and served them with
two knobs of butter. As I sank my teeth into the succulent
yellow cob for the first time, my stomach churned. The
fact that I was in the second month of pregnancy, and
had never tasted this food before, didn't help. For me it
was totally unpalatable and I was violently sick. I discarded corn on the cob because, after twenty-three years
without it in my diet, and at a difficult physical time, it
was not palatable.

Something similar was true of the gift of 'tongues'.
Many and varied subjects had been covered in my
church and all were part of a healthy spiritual diet which
caused my strong growth in the Christian life. The
spiritual gifts such as prophecy, dreams, visions, tongues
and interpretation, and healing were not part of our
spiritual menu. Not surprisingly, after such a fulfilled
upbringing, I turned my nose up in ignorance at these
seemingly unsavoury ingredients. They were obviously
not essential to my salvation, nor were they needed for
my growth thus far, so what was all the fuss about? Just
thinking about the unknown increased my insecurity and
homesickness in my first month at college, so it was
easier to dismiss it out of order.

If ever I ask Doug what he would like to eat, sweetcorn or corn-on-the-cob is usually included on the menu.
As a result, I have grown accustomed to the smell and
taste of corn, and although it is not essential to my diet, I
now enjoy it and the proteins build me up. All human
illustrations fall down somewhere and my occasional
enjoyment of sweetcorn is totally inadequate for describ-
ing my growing understanding of the gift of 'tongues' and
my eventual use of it.

My work in evangelism and teaching has led to events
with Christians from different backgrounds and persua-
sions. God has opened my mind and heart and given me
opportunities not only to hear this subject unpacked

from Scripture by gifted teachers, but also to see and hear it in action. Patient explanation of controversial phrases has been appreciated, and God's reassurance throughout it all led me to read many books on the subject.

The book which was the means by which God untied my last knot of resistance was *You are my God* by David Watson. This is not a book specifically about 'tongues', but one that plots the author's journey in a relationship with his God. I identified with him in his struggle with this area of prayer and avidly read his realistic, down-to-earth comments: 'I suppose I was expecting God to waggle my tongue so that the words would rush out. But it never happened to me like that.' I had sat many times with open mouth, asking God to fill it with the gift of 'tongues'. I had heard so many mystifying comments such as 'The sounds just came,' and 'It wasn't me, it was from God.' My bewilderment only increased. David Watson continued: 'Later, I was impressed by Luke's statement in Acts 2 verse 4—"they began to speak in other tongues as the Spirit gave them utterance." They had to do the speaking.' I could not be passive in this receiving of a gift. I must accept it and speak it. There was no doubt God was highlighting my need for this particular gift. I struggled when praying for the unknown or for people whose specific needs I didn't fully understand. My mounting excitement about praise and worship was often limited by the English language. In times of fear or extreme tension, the word 'help' seemed increasingly inadequate for the growing realisation that God answers and protects us. Then there were those times when I felt so unutterably weary and weak that I didn't know what to ask God for personally. Oh for a perfect language that prayed right to the heart of a situation or need! A language that doesn't make our native tongue redundant but enriches it and works with it in strengthening our communication with God and our fellow human beings.

As I continued to search Scripture and read books, I came across another observation that followed on from David Watson's practical comment on Acts 2:4. In his book *Keep in Step with the Spirit*, Dr J.I. Packer, on the subject of speaking in tongues, says, 'Whether one's first entry into it was spontaneous and involuntary, or by learning a vocal technique for it (both happen), does not affect its devotional value once one can manage it.' Obviously, I was not in the first category that J.I. Packer talked about in his book. I hadn't had a spontaneous and involuntary experience of speaking in tongues, as many do. The other alternative was to learn a vocal technique. Having previously asked God to teach me to pray, I now just added the two words 'in tongues'. Having learned so much that was new in the previous few years, I was hungry for whatever God had for me, and by now I was discovering that God made room for my trial and error.

Just as a child has to experiment in walking, talking and eating, and parents stand by to help, so our loving Father stands by to guide, encourage and pick us up in our exercising of spiritual gifts. We learn nothing new unless we launch out and try. As on that first day of learning to ski, I felt vulnerable. Was I going to make a fool of myself? I was seated behind the wheel of my car, one of my favourite places for prayer. The engine was humming, my eyes, hands and feet were occupied, so why not occupy my voice with sounds I was not used to? I was accustomed to humming and singing along with the radio or a tape, so I found it easier to release these sounds while singing. The more I listened to the sound with my human ear, the more stupid I felt! However, when I offered them to God and concentrated on him, I was unexpectedly encouraged. Was this what Paul meant when he wrote: 'He who speaks in tongues edifies himself' (1 Cor 14:4)? That first drive into the unknown led to walks where I was not only refreshed but renewed spiritually as the use of tongues gave me an alertness and concentration in prayer never experienced before. I would alternate between English and 'tongues', and found with the latter that it was a good short-cut when needing to pray for several things.

To avoid inferring laziness, let me give you an example. In May 1986, the churches of Wessex united for an outreach mission held in the Bournemouth International Centre entitled 'He's Here!'. Ian Coffey was the main speaker, and members from the mission team had gathered for prayer before the main meeting. The massive Windsor Hall was filling up rapidly and nervous tension was mounting. My mind was a tangle of confused needs which I was finding difficult to express to God. Having been behind the scenes on so many of these occasions, I knew the extreme pressure on a speaker. A number of my friends would be present who needed prayer. I was concerned for the Saltmine Theatre Company and others taking part in the programme.

All these concerns, and many more, jostled for my attention as I joined the hundreds of people in the auditorium. As Ian got up to speak, I felt compelled to pray for him through every word. Silently I prayed in tongues. The exercise of the gift prevented my mind from wandering and caused such participation in the message that my heart was pounding as if I were up there preaching. At the same time, I realised that God could take those silent words and apply them wherever necessary. He knew the needs of every heart in that huge auditorium and could interpret my prayer for those specific areas. As Ian closed with prayer, I realised that my mind had not wandered once. All the time that I had been praying for others, God, at the same time, had applied his word to my heart. When we pray in our own language we can only ask or pray for one thing at a time. On occasions such as 'He's Here!', God's gift of tongues can discipline our minds, concentrate our thoughts, and channel our prayer. How powerful and economical our God is!

I cannot fully understand the gift of tongues, but God is teaching me how to use it. I am learning that his gifts are not toys to play with but tools he equips us with. In using a tool, or any piece of modern machinery, it is vital that the expert be alongside us, showing us the correct and most effective way of operating it. Disregarding the maker's instructions can lead to bewilderment, frustration and, in some cases, disastrous consequences. The same is true of the gifts given by God. We need the Holy Spirit to come alongside us and guide us into all truth (Jn 16:30). My first use of an industrial orbital sander on our open-plan staircase effectively taught me how stupid I was—I tried to operate it manually, not waiting for the expert's advice, and ended in a frustrated heap. In the hands of the expert, and operated by the power of electricity, I was later to see and allowed to experience for myself how very effective that sander is. If I had been left in my ignorance, that tool would have been unattractive, heavy and cumbersome, and I would have failed to see of what use it was to me.

Over the years, inadequate or non-existent teaching and the abuse of certain of these more demonstrative gifts has caused many of us to shy away from the use of tongues in our relationship with God. I have found that just as the industrial orbital sander was not rendered non-existent or ineffective just because I operated it incorrectly, so what God says to us in Scripture about the gift of tongues should not be ignored or dismissed as not for today, just because of the non-use or abuse of recent years. Paul, in his wisdom, knew how much more noticable and disruptive is the abuse of a gift and gives some clear directions for the right use of gifts in the church in 1 Corinthians 14:26–33. Speaking as one who used the gift of tongues himself, he knew that alongside those who abuse the gift, are the many who quietly and effectively use the gift for themselves and for the strengthening of the whole church.

Tongues have proved to be an effective gift at times of extreme emotion—joy, fear, suffering, dread, panic and thankfulness. God's economic language bypasses our human limitations and deals with, and aids us, through each situation. It is in these extreme times of trial that Peter reminds us: 'So be truly glad. There is wonderful joy ahead, even if the going is rough for a while down here. These trials are only to test your faith, to see whether or not it is strong and pure. It is being tested as fire tests gold and purifies it—and your faith is far more precious to God than mere gold. So if your faith remains strong after being tried in the test tube of fiery trials, it will bring you much praise and glory and honour on the day of his return' (1 Pet 1:6–7, TLB). In my relationship with God, it has been through the test-tube of fiery trials that I have learned most about total reliance on him.

It was in one of these demanding situations that God spoke clearly to me through the prayer warrior, Daniel. So often we cry out, not knowing how to ask for a situation. Daniel 9 and 10 tell us that Daniel fasted and prayed for three weeks to help him understand his situation and that of his nation. Our communication is often rendered useless because of our lack of perspective on and understanding of the entire circumstances. We have a test-tube eye view of the predicament, distorted by the turbulent bubbles of panic, that needs God's reassuring, calming perspective and presence. That takes time and discipline. The example of Daniel in taking time to get God's perspective and understanding before praying to the heart of the circumstance has changed my whole approach to prayer. Fasting has had an increasing effect not only on my approach to prayer, but also my appreciation of God. His progressive teaching and guidance in this area of prayer, where actions back up our words, is alerting me to his perspective and understanding of our relationship and its purpose.

In Matthew 6:16, Jesus links fasting with his teaching on giving and praying. 'When you fast' assumes that this discipline is all part of our relationship with God. It is by no means a command but, like tongues, an invitation to explore another area of discipline which can enhance and strengthen our communication with God.

More direct words come from Jesus in Matthew 9:15, in answer to the Pharisees' critical questions. From their rigid and legalistic position, they seek to trip Jesus up through his disciples' lack of fasting. His immediate reply is, 'Can the wedding guests mourn as long as the bridegroom is with them? The days will come when the bridegroom is taken from them, and then they will fast.' Jesus in bodily presence was very much with them.

He had quietly entered this world, breaking a 400 year silence since Malachi foretold his coming. In our Bibles, it is just the distance of two flimsy pages between the first verses of Malachi 3 and Matthew 2: 'Then suddenly the Lord you are seeking will come to his temple, the messenger of the covenant you desire will come says the Lord almighty' (Mal 3:1). 'Jesus was born in the town of Bethlehem of Judea' (Mt 2:1). What a difference those few pages make! With the coming of Jesus, a new age had begun. The Messiah, the bridegroom, was right there with them—Emmanuel, God with us. It was a time of celebration and feasting, not mourning and fasting. There would be a time for the disciples to fast, but not bound by the old law. Those days would be when Jesus was taken from them. As Arthur Wallis clearly states in his book *God's Chosen Fast*: 'We are, therefore, compelled to refer the days of his absence to the period of this age, from the time he ascended to the Father until he shall return from heaven.' This is, evidently, how Jesus' apostles understood him, for it was not until after his ascension to the Father that we read of them fasting—'It is this age of the church to which our master referred when he said, then they will fast, the time is now' (Acts 13:2–3).

I could not escape those powerful words and set out to learn as much as I could on the subject. I have met people who have highlighted individual values and reasons for fasting, such as specific guidance, concentration for prolonged periods of prayer, deliverance, interpretation of dreams, preparation for speaking, and physical and spiritual cleansing. I am discovering these are all secondary reasons to the primary purpose for fasting which is to deepen our relationship with God. We need to heed the cry from God's heart in Zechariah 7:5—'When you fasted, was it really for me you fasted?' If God is not initiating the fast, it will simply be a self-motivated attempt to twist God's arm into action. At best it will be a pointless exercise of frustration, and at worst an ego boost. There are some natural parallels between the physical and spiritual exercise of fasting, which can help us in our relationship with God.

First, fasting is a 'clearout operation'. Over a longer fast, which should be worked towards gradually, the first few days can be uncomfortable as the body begins to rid itself of toxins that have built up over years of bad eating. Some who for medical reasons cannot and should not attempt long fasts, find one regular day a week is sufficient for a good rest and clearout of the system. I find that this spiritual time of fasting also brings to the surface those impurities which control us. We cover up what lies inside with food and other good things. By depriving ourselves of one of these masks, we allow God to bring to the surface the pride, anger, bitterness, a critical spirit, jealousy or fear—whatever lurks there controlling us. All of these and many others build up over years of complacent, ill-disciplined living—we need a regular, God-initiated 'clearout'.

Secondly, it is a feast as well as a fast. By doing without food physically and feeding on God's word spiritually, we are forcibly reminded of the disastrous consequences of permanently giving up food. How often we neglect the word of God and wonder why we falter in our faith and our prayers are paralysed. The initial touch of dizziness reminds us how spiritually disorientated we will become if not feeding on God's word.

Thirdly, through a period of fasting, whatever the length, God brings his perspective and balance to our lives. As we are continually reminded of this special and concentrated time with God, we discover how petty non-essentials creep in to dominate our lives, bringing a crazy imbalance. By allowing God to open our eyes to his priorities, and in presenting our minds as well as our bodies to God, we start discovering the practical truth of Romans 12:2—'Do not conform any longer to the pattern of this world, but be transformed by the renewing of your mind. Then you will be able to test and approve what God's will is—his good, pleasing and perfect will.' As I glimpse what is on God's heart, so I am able to pray within his will, which can be completely different to what I was going to request at the outset of the period of prayer.

Six years ago my friend and prayer partner Ruth lost her husband John. This sudden trauma drew us closer as we continually prayed through each obstacle that presented itself. This courageous mother, son and daughter continued to run their family business on which the neighbourhood depended so much. It soon became clear, because of Ruth's health, that the business would have to be sold. This was an urgent need, but the market was slow. We had decided to have a weekly day's fast. Monday was convenient as I could usually join her at the shop. In between customers, of whom there were many, we would urge God to supply the right buyer and ask for a smooth and rapid sale. As the weeks passed, there was no sign of an answer. We were puzzled and very disappointed when a transaction fell through at the last minute. Still we continued our weekly fast, slowly realising that God has a hidden agenda and timetable for this situation and we had much to learn about understanding his ways. Our day's fast was now affecting our prayer for the rest of the week, and after twelve weeks we both felt, against all odds, and with no outward evidence, that God had answered our prayer, that we should be thanking him instead of pleading with him. It was through the observation of Ruth's daughter Karen that we continued our fast. 'Surely,' she said, with her down-to-earth wisdom, 'if you took twelve weeks to fast and pray for something, you should take at least that period of time in thanking him!' God was using Karen to speak directly to us. That period of thanksgiving with fasting was an education for both of us. It raised our expectation of what God was going to do, it deepened our trust in him when we could not depend on outward signs of progress, and we learned to love him for himself. We were not to see the answer to our initial prayer for another twelve months. In our relationship with God, he answered many far more important needs as a result of that time with him.

Our love for God is so dependent on what he can do for us and tends to lose its intensity when God has answered our prayers and things are going well. Hosea spoke of God's yearning for our unconditional love: 'Your love for me disappears as quickly as morning mist; it is like dew that vanishes early in the day. ... What I want from you is plain and clear: I want your constant love' (Hos 6:4–6, GNB).

In all physical exercise, it is vital to build up stamina gradually, so in our food-orientated society the spiritual exercise of fasting should be embarked upon sensibly and progressively. There are those who, for physical reasons, should not fast. Expectant mothers, those breast-feeding their babies, diabetics, heart patients and those who are prone to anorexia. If in doubt over any physical condition, always gain medical advice. Jesus practised fasting as a discipline for all his life, and so we see his incredible marathon of fasting which stretched for forty days. God is not so interested in the length of a physical exercise, but in the love of a spiritual attitude. Those who for medical or other reasons decide fasting is not for them, can apply the central ideal in fasting to other areas of life. In fasting, we willingly deny ourselves a normal need or function to concentrate on God and his purpose. It is good to examine our day or week and observe those things we have come to need—perhaps a normal routine or regular pastime. Many of them are enjoyable and wholesome, but it would cost us to withdraw from them for a period of time to highlight our overriding need for God. What about the television, the radio, sleep, friends, a favourite sport? Our list could get longer, but unless our relationship with God gets deeper, fasting just becomes a self-centred piece of exhibitionism. It is no wonder that Jesus gave suggestions for behaviour throughout fasting 'so that it will not be obvious to men that you are fasting, but only to your Father' (Mt 6:16–18).

Workout session

Alone

(1) Read Nehemiah 1:4–11
     Esther 4:12–17
     Luke 4:1–13
     Acts 13:1–3
     Acts 14:19–23.

Note down the motivation and different circumstances for these fasts.

(2) Try fasting from television, radio or your newspaper for one week. Note your reaction and lessons learned. N.B. Fasting extends to video recording for this week as well!

(3) Is there an area in prayer you need to ask God to teach you about? Don't forget simply to ask. Read Matthew 7:7–11.

In groups

(1) Share your first reaction to the thought of fasting.

(2) Discuss what value fasting could have in your daily life. Eg, business, family.

(3) As a group, explore the area of fasting from the media. Feed back what you learn about God and yourself.

(4) Discuss how tears can be a language heard, understood and treasured by God.

(5) In pairs, highlight the area you would like God to teach you more about: tears, tongues or fasting. Pray for each other for that specific need.

Recommended reading

David Watson, *You Are My God* (Hodder and Stoughton: London)
George Mallone, *Those Controversial Gifts* (Hodder and Stoughton: London)
Richard Foster, *Celebration of Discipline*, including study guide, (Hodder and Stoughton: London)

11

Danger—Men at Work

I was captured by the commotion and confusion. An atmosphere reminiscent of holiday excitement permeated the chaotic building site, with workers of all ages and both sexes joking in their activity. Not a helmet or piece of protective clothing was in sight as heavy equipment and building materials were carried in all directions with no apparent co-ordination. Picking their precarious way through the rubble came two men carrying a long beam of wood. From the attention given to the beam it was obvious that it was a key part of the structure, and it was raised high to be placed in position. All eyes watched as the two men laughed at their ineffective attempt to position the beam on shaking bricks and incomplete foundations.

I was choked by anxiety over the danger of the

situation, with so many upturned, unprotected heads beneath and unconcerned children playing innocently in a fools' paradise of bricks and dust, unaware of any overhead disaster. Without warning the cumbersome beam slipped and, as if in slow motion, hung dangerously in the air, before crashing to the ground.

The breath I had been holding in anxiety was expelled in a gasp as I surfaced from sleep, never to see the outcome of my dream. I snatched up a pen and my prayer diary; the words ringing in my ears were far clearer than the fading dream: 'Except the Lord build the house, they labour in vain that build it' (Ps 127:1, AV)

It was 7.30am and all was quiet before the onslaught of the day. Never before had I experienced this urgent need to capture a fast-fading dream on paper, but because of its strong link with Scripture, I had to check whether God might be speaking to me through the silence and stillness of sleep.

I knew God had spoken powerfully in the past to people through dreams and visions. The Josephs of the Old and New Testaments are clear examples. One was to be Prime Minister of Egypt, the other the earthly father of Jesus. I had read of many ordinary people since Bible days, who down through the ages had heard God's voice through dreams. But right now on Friday 16th of June at 7.30 in the morning, it was a different matter! My mind sped back to my simple, continual prayer over the years, 'Lord, teach me to pray.' He was teaching me to explore every area of communication with him, not just to depend on others' opinions and experiences, as helpful as these can be, but to have first-hand knowledge and experience from God himself. As the kettle started to boil on that warm June morning, and with my eyes still blurred with sleep, I wrote, 'Father ... before anything else, help me to capture on paper my dream and if it is from you ... confirm it!' Eighteen months have passed since that request was written. Months of prayer, heart-searching, learning of continual lessons and, above all, the peace that God gave the dream and is still speaking to me through it.

As I memorised the first verse of Psalm 127 that accompanied the dream, I realised the importance of memorising Scripture. The words that had come so forcibly were from the Authorised Version learned so long ago as a child. I now completed that verse and committed it to memory afresh from the New International Version: 'Unless the Lord builds the house, its builders labour in vain. Unless the Lord watches over the city, the watchmen stand guard in vain.'

God started to apply Scripture and the visual aid of my dream to the foundations and building of our family and home. In the dream I had eventually seen that the structure being built was a church. But I knew God was also speaking to me concerning my own Christian life and my family. The apparent enjoyment and lack of co-ordination could easily be seen over recent years. I had thoroughly enjoyed building our home and family in the early years, treating the long separations from Doug as a challenge, although we had our fair share of tough times. I proudly took on the role of mother and father, often having to head up the family in Doug's absence. As time passed, challenge upon challenge captured our attention. So often our plans and decisions were sucking us into a round of activity. Although we consulted with God, there was never time to wait for his answers. Through my dream God graphically described my heart and is now helping me to sort out my priorities, shed surplus activity not of him, and rebuild the foundations and walls of our family.

Five months after the dream, Doug had a three-month sabbatical. It was so refreshing to be at home as a family, and we had plenty of opportunities to pray and talk together. Through the years of ministry and travel, this all-important foundation of our marriage and family had been crowded out. A study of Nehemiah reminded us of the many practical details involved in rebuilding and structuring. First came Nehemiah's four months of preparation, including prayer and fasting, before he approached the king concerning the great walls of Jerusalem. Then came the extensive and intricate examination. He walked personally around the walls of the city at night to avoid attracting attention and interruption. As he walked and scrutinised, God put in his heart those things that needed to be built up, repaired, cleared of clutter or renewed.

Gradually God unravelled my dream as we compared Psalm 127:1 with those verses in Nehemiah concerning laying foundations, building and protecting. So much of the building in our marriage, homes, families, churches and societies depends on manpower and neglects God's power to create and direct in all the practical areas. As I examined the structure of our family life, walked around our activities and relationships, gained perspective on our church life and work around the country, God probed beneath the cosmetic activity to deal with my foundational relationship with him. People had to be put before programmes, family before the filofax and prayer before performance.

With the breakdown of so many homes and relationships, and with the crises that many churches are facing throughout the country, we need courageous men and women who will stop the frantic round of activity and return to the costly times of prayer and fasting to find out what God is feeling and saying about our relationships, homes, families, churches and nation.

Several months after my dream, God focused my thoughts on the last part of Psalm 127:1, 'Unless the Lord watches over the city, the watchmen stand guard in vain.' How little I knew of spiritual warfare and the exercise of watching over my family and church in this age of evil and violence. We need people with these specific gifts to stand guard in prayer and watch over the life and activity of the church. Because of their gift, they will have perspective from God, and will be able to stand in protection over leaders and members and speak right into situations.

Where my family was concerned, I started praying with more urgency for protection. God knows all about their future partners and children, about careers and imminent crises, and it is vital to get praying early about these unseen areas. Remembering the vulnerable, unprotected heads in my dream, I prayed for protective clothing and armour (see Col 3; Eph 6). Our Western, twentieth-century minds expect things to run smoothly, but we would be better equipped if we had a realistic approach that expected tough times, was prepared for them, and was ready to learn through them.

Being filled with the Spirit is an intensely practical daily exercise—one in which we ask God to fill, equip and protect us with his effective resources for life's bitter battles as well as its successes. When we face teenage tyranny, let's ask for his understanding love and wisdom; when opposition and criticism at work or in the church come our way, we need his serene acceptance rather than our retaliation. His quiet resolve can drive out feelings of defeat and loneliness, and heartache can be soothed by his love and healing. This is no wishful thinking, but the basic outworking of being filled with the Spirit. God commands it and longs to do it for us, but he needs our continual co-operation. As Paul wrote: 'Be being filled' (Eph 5:18). It is a continual exercise, building the muscles of endurance and victory.

All this and still more to come from one dream. How understanding and imaginative God is in his communication with us. I have given over to God this whole area of

visual images in the mind, whether in dreams while
asleep or pictures and visions while awake. God created
all these areas; to some he speaks in one area, to others
in a completely different one. It is important to develop
sensitive hearts and minds which recognise his voice and
discern his methods.

I am slowly discovering, with a God who makes room
for my trial and error, how to test what is of him or what
is rooted in self; when it is his voice and not my hopes or
fears; when it is his prompting and not others' persua-
sion. The Bible clearly warns against false dreams,
prophets and visions: 'Indeed, I am against those who
prophecy false dreams,' declares the Lord. 'They tell
them and lead the people astray with their reckless lies,
yet I did not send them or appoint them. They do not
benefit these people in the least' declares the Lord.
(Jer 23:32). Similar warnings are repeated elsewhere in
Scripture (Eg, Ezek 27:9; 13:3–7).

So how can we be sure a dream, vision or picture is of
God? First, does it agree with Scripture? The visions
of Joseph Smith upon which Mormonism is founded
contradict Scripture. The same is true of Christian
Science, whose founder Mary Baker-Eddy taught that
sin and death are mere illusions, totally contrary to the
teaching of Scripture. John Newton however was warned
by God in a dream before his conversion, not to neglect
the grace of God, and was later to write that Bible-based
hymn Amazing Grace, a perfect example of a dream
agreeing with Scripture.

So what of my dream? Dreams are not always accompanied by a verse of Scripture. I am so thankful to
God that the verse has stayed with me more powerfully
than the dream. Within seconds of waking it sent me to
search the Psalms and commit it to memory. In fact in
the last eighteen months it has been the springboard for
many studies in the rest of Scripture on such subjects as

building, labouring in vain, watchmen, leaders and team work. The unfolding of the dream has caused me to study the Bible with more determination.

Second, does the vision or dream cause us to understand and to love God more and draw us closer to him? The early morning episode back in June drove all thoughts of cups of tea and making sandwiches out of my mind. My first thoughts are still written in a hasty scrawl: 'Father ... before anything else ... help me!' Tough lessons have been learned, difficult directions have been obeyed, sometimes too slowly, but in retrospect God has drawn me closer to him through it all. I wouldn't have chosen this route, but his ways are perfect. Not always comfortable, but definitely perfect!

Third, does the dream or vision lead to peace in following through God's direction, or does it result in panic, fear or depression? The accuracy and fulfilment of a dream alone does not prove its divine origin. In Deuteronomy 13:1–5 we read a warning against prophets whose words come to pass but who say, 'Let us go after other gods.' God's communication to me through the dream has spoken peace and security into some extremely difficult times. However, the whole area of the insecure structure and the beam falling causes concern as I travel. So many churches are experiencing major leadership and structural problems, families are struggling with guiding and caring, and increasing numbers of Christians are finding that their foundations are being tested by the demanding days in which we live. Are we building sandcastles as the tide draws dangerously close, or is God the builder?

Fourth, it is important to check that there has been no contact with the occult. This might have been in the past, or more recent, but however slight or serious it must be repented of. The devil loves to counterfeit God's work.

Fifth, does the message draw attention to the giver? Is

it a spiritual status symbol? The danger is to seek visions and dreams for their own sake, not for the building up of others and for God's glory.

Sixth, where possible it is good to give the dream or vision the test of time, thus gaining confirmation through other means, such as Scripture, circumstances, prayer partners and other prophecies. In the early days I shared the intricate details of my dream with Doug and two other close prayer partners. Later, it was good to share it with someone right out of our area and situation to gain their wisdom and perspective.

Lastly, if wider action is needed it should be submitted to Christian leadership. This should be done sensitively and submissively, for testing and interpretation. The Holy Spirit is the expert in interpretation and will help to discern the source and purpose of communication through the body of Christ, which is his people exercising his gifts.

Many dreams must have flashed across the screen of my mind but I remember very few. I have written down one other dream, and following the test list above, I have rapidly eliminated it as not being a message from God. There are those who regularly communicate God's word through dreams or visions and who have developed a keen discernment for God's voice, while I struggle with one dream! How important it is not to covet or selfishly compare, but to learn from one another and revel in every discovery we make that draws us closer to God.

All the areas of prayer I have explored with you are incomplete, as they are part of an ongoing relationship with a God who takes time and has infinite patience with those he teaches. Until I see him face to face I will continue to learn, and make mistakes because as Paul says, 'We can see and understand only a little about God now, as if we were peering at his reflection in a poor mirror; but some day we are going to see him in his completeness, face to face. Now all that I know is hazy and blurred, but then I will see everything clearly, just as clearly as God sees into my heart right now. There are three things that remain—faith, hope and love—and the greatest of these is love. Let love be your greatest aim' (1 Cor 13:12, TLB).

Recommended reading

David Watson, *You Are My God* (Hodder and Stoughton: London)

David Pytches, *Come Holy Spirit* (Hodder and Stoughton: London)

James I Packer, *Keep in Step with the Spirit* (IVP: Leicester)

George Mallone, *Those Controversial Gifts* (Hodder and Stoughton: London)

John White, *When the Spirit Comes with Power* (Hodder and Stoughton: London)

Richard Foster, *Celebration of Discipline*, and Study Guide (Hodder and Stoughton: London)

Postscript

The chapters were finished, the final illustration penned. Editing had been tiring and I breathed a sigh of relief as I packed everything I would need for my final computer session before the deadline. Belinda, my computer expert, had patiently deciphered my demented dictation on the numerous tapes I had given her. Her accuracy and sense of humour kept me sane when my tired mind went into overdrive. She and Mick were expecting their second baby, and with a change of Mick's job they had moved up to the Midlands. Their home was my destination, starting at 6am from Bournemouth to drive 200 miles up country. Months before when they left our area the computer disk and ribbon had been returned to me. Laying them to one side I guarded the white box, with the disk in it, with my life. It represented nine chapters of blood, sweat and tears!

The journey through mounting traffic was made without hold-up. I was relieved to unload the computer, disk, tapes, notes and myself into Belinda's home. All was present and correct, and we could get down to business. Catching up on all our news, I didn't notice Belinda's puzzled look as she cast her eye over the equipment. I was waxing eloquent over their latest arrival, Stephanie, when Belinda's hesitant request cut me short. 'Sue, where's the disk?' I pointed to the white box I had placed on the computer. 'No,' she said patiently, 'the floppy disk, Sue, with all the chapters on it?' There was a mounting urgency in her voice. I laughed at her desperate face and gave her the treasured box. 'Don't worry Belinda, this is the very last thing I would have forgotten. I have been guarding it with my life.' She sat down suddenly and whispered, 'No, Sue—that is a computer ribbon!'

Realisation gradually seeped into my mind. For seven months I had treasured and guarded a ribbon. A very important part of the computer and therefore of my book, but not the real thing. I had laid that down somewhere, and I couldn't remember where or when. Panic seized me as I struggled to grasp the implications of our dilemma. Should I return South and search? What if it had been thrown away? I had no recollection of receiving anything else besides the white box, let alone remembering where I put it!

As I made that three-hour return journey, my mind was in turmoil. Everything I had written and agonised over swung into urgent, untidy action. I poured out my desperation to God as I raced down the M5. Why had he allowed me to be under such a misconception over all this time? Out of all my tangled prayer came two clear requests. The first was that my mind and body would stay fresh and alert for the marathon drive. Secondly, that if the disk was at home, I would go straight to its hiding place. If answered, both prayers would be miracles. Not only had I risen at 5am that morning, but I had been writing and editing throughout several previous nights. As for the whereabouts of the disk, our house has walls covered with books and drawers packed with equipment. It would take hours of searching which could end in futility.

I found the disk. I completed the drive of 600 miles. The book was finally finished. But that day will stay in my memory for what God spoke through my ignorance and stupidity.

The most precious person in our lives is God. The most precious possession is our relationship with him. The problem is that we so often guard the things we think are him. Our position in church, our family, our ministry, our gifts, book-writing, sermon preparation, meeting-going, conference attendance and committees. All these and so much more are important and are part of our relationship with God. But they are not the real thing. God often gets crowded out by all the activity that so often replaces our spirituality. The danger is that we don't realise we have abandoned him and don't have time to remember when or where. What would your reply be if you were stopped in your tracks, as Belinda stopped me, and someone demanded of you, 'Where is your God? Where is your relationship with him?' Do we dare take a costly trip back to where we deserted him, or has our activity and position become our security? My request 'Lord, teach me to pray' started my journey back—and then onwards—in a continuous relationship which is central to my life. Paul's prayer sums up my desire for us all:

I ask God from the wealth of his glory to give you power through his Spirit to be strong in your inner selves, and I pray that Christ will make his home in your hearts through faith. I pray that you may have your roots and foundation in love, so that you, together with all God's people, may have the power to understand how broad and long, how high and deep, is Christ's love. Yes, may you come to know his love—although it can never be fully known—and so be completely filled with the very nature of God.

To him *who by means of his power working in us* is able to do so much more that we can ever ask for, or even think of: to God be the glory in the church and in Christ Jesus for all time, for ever and ever! AMEN!' (Eph 3:16–21, GNB, my italics).

Prayer of commitment

Lord Jesus

I know that I am a sinner and need your forgiveness.

I believe that you died for my sins and I want to turn from them.

I now invite you to come into my life by your Holy Spirit.

Be my Saviour and Lord and make me the kind of person you want me to be.

Amen.

The Believer's Guide To Spiritual Warfare

by Tom White

How to resist the devil through hand-to-hand combat in the spiritual realm.

What is spiritual warfare, and who should be engaged in it?

How do we join battle? What are our weapons?

Tom White made a pledge to God when he became a Christian that he would help others remain free of the Enemy that nearly destroyed his life. *The Believer's Guide to Spiritual Warfare* will help you to:

- deal with oppression
- resist temptation
- pray effectively for your family
- break curses
- cleanse places
- distinguish the demonic from the psychological, emotional and physical

and much, much more.

'Those who take Satan seriously, and the victory of Jesus even more seriously, would be well advised to take this book seriously as well.'

PETER LAWRENCE
Vicar of Christ Church,
Burney Lane, Birmingham

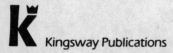

Kingsway Publications